Weightlifting for Teenagers

Author: Jacob Nelson, B.S. Exercise Science, NASM, ACSM-EP
Editor: Mary Dieterich
Proofreaders: Alexis Fey and April Hawkins

ISBN 978-1-62223-910-8

Printing No. CD-405096

Mark Twain Media, Inc., Publishers
Distributed by Carson Dellosa Education

Visit us at www.marktwainpublishing.com

Table of Contents

Introduction

Weightlifting for Teenagers is designed to give teenagers a basic understanding of the fundamentals of **weightlifting**, including but not limited to, exercise selection, how to resistance-train safely and avoid injury, how to progressive overload, how to structure exercise programs, and to give a broad view of the key fundamentals that will help build lifelong habits to improve their health and wellness. Young adults have the benefit of recovering very quickly from exercise and making tremendous strides in muscle growth and development. By using this book to help get them started in their lifelong pursuit of fitness, they will build the foundational habits to help ensure success in the weight room.

One of the hardest parts of starting an exercise program is not knowing where to start and being extremely anxious to walk into a gym for the first time not knowing anything. Hopefully, with the modernization of many Physical Education classes, many high schools will have at least a semester of resistance training that should expose teenagers to **free weights** and some **weightlifting machines**. Unfortunately, these students might not always have access to a knowledgeable trainer to show them the basics.

The goal of this book is to help teenagers understand the basic rules and fundamentals of resistance training to help them build the right habits at a young age so those habits stick with them for the rest of their lives. This book not only will help you learn how to exercise, but truly understand the goals and purpose of resistance training in hopes that students will fall in love with the never-ending pursuit of growth. Weightlifting encourages and builds a **growth mindset**, which is the belief that a person's most basic abilities can be developed through dedication and hard work. Success depends on time and effort. The more time and effort you give to something, the better you get at it. Weightlifting is great because the more time and energy you put in, the stronger, faster, and more muscular you will become. It teaches the value of hard work and investing in yourself. You will only live in one body, so treat it like a temple and you will live in a beautiful home for the rest of your life—something no one can take away from you.

Use this book as your lighthouse in your journey, keeping you on track with the fundamentals and basic rules of resistance training. Refer back to it when you inevitably run into issues, whether that may be small aches and pains, hitting a plateau in the gym, or educating friends, family members, or even teachers on the benefits of resistance training. For the purpose of this book, *weightlifting* and *resistance training* will both be used interchangeably. As the name implies, **weightlifting** is a type of exercise that involves lifting weights as added resistance. **Resistance** is placed on your muscles and that stimulates strength and muscle growth adaptations. The stronger you get, the more weight you need to add to get those same growth adaptations. **Resistance training** simply means you are exercising with resistance, which is typically weights or bands. These two terms will be used interchangeably throughout the book.

Chapter 1: Principles of Resistance Training

Weightlifting follows a very specific set of principles that can be difficult to understand at first, but become easy once you wrap your head around them. **Weightlifting**, or **resistance training**, is a form of physical activity designed to improve muscular fitness, including strength, size, and endurance. Weightlifting is one of the oldest forms of exercise. In ancient Greece, athletes would use weights made of stone and metal to push, pull, squat, and lift in order to make themselves stronger, faster, and bigger. They understood that by adding MORE weight than what they weigh by themselves, they could make their muscles even bigger, stronger, and develop greater feats of athleticism. Today, weightlifting is the most common method of exercise for most major sports, including football, basketball, baseball, soccer, rugby, and even endurance running. Resistance training not only makes muscles stronger, but makes the body more resilient and less likely to get injured. Resistance training also lowers the risk of cardiovascular disease, diabetes, stroke, Alzheimer's, and many other diseases. Weightlifting is the **longevity**, or anti-aging, pill that you can only take by devoting your own time and effort to it. In order for you to benefit from weightlifting, you must first understand the most basic principle of resistance training—progressive overload.

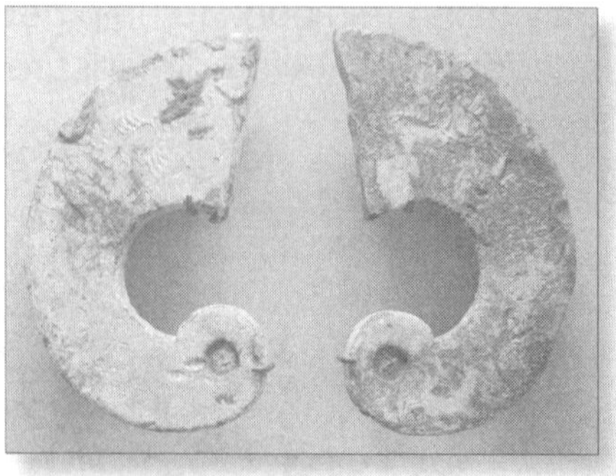

Weights used by ancient Greeks while they were jumping

Progressive Overload

Progressive overload is the act of gradually boosting the intensity of your workout over time. In order to improve physical fitness or reach the stimulus level to achieve physical adaptations, the body must undergo greater demands over time. To make progress in strength, endurance, or muscle size, you must gradually increase intensity, duration, frequency, and/or volume beyond what your current level of fitness is.

When you apply the progressive overload principle to your workouts, you are pushing your body slightly beyond its comfort zone. The workout is called a **stimulus**, and by increasing the intensity of the stimulus, your body responds by improving strength, increasing muscle size, improving its cardiovascular performance, and/or gaining more flexibility. In other words, if you want to build strength, you must gradually increase the amount you are lifting over time. If you want to gain muscle size, you must gradually increase weight, repetitions, or volume over time. If you want to improve your cardiovascular endurance, you must run farther, run faster, or run on an incline. If you want to gain flexibility, you have to stretch your muscles over a greater range of motion over time. If you want to get physically and mentally stronger in life, you have to undergo some degree of stress.

As you increase the intensity, duration, frequency, or volume of the stimulus, you increase your level of fitness.

Chapter 1: Principles of Resistance Training (cont.)

The Greeks had a phenomenal story to help understand this principle. Milo of Croton was a famous Greek athlete who lived in the Greek colony of Croton in what is now Italy. There are many stories surrounding this Olympian athlete, but the only one that describes progressive overload depicts a story of him carrying his calf. The story goes that when Milo was a young boy, he was given a calf to feed and take care of. Every day, he would have to throw this calf on his shoulders and hike it up a mountain to feed and water it. In the beginning, he was a small boy carrying a small calf. It was hard work the first day, but as he ate well and rested that night, he found himself even stronger the next day, making it a little easier to carry the calf. His body grew muscle in his legs and upper body from hiking up the mountain carrying the calf. Now, as he grew, so too did the calf. The calf got bigger every day, so even though Milo was also getting bigger, this was still tiresome work because the calf would get heavier. Milo grew as the calf grew; his body had to in order to continue carrying the calf up the mountain. After four years of carrying the calf up the mountain, he realized he wasn't carrying a calf any longer, but a bull! By this time, Milo was incredibly strong and this led to all his Olympic glory. Most importantly, this story summarizes progressive overload in action. You need to constantly increase the demands you impose on your muscles so that they continually adapt and grow. In this case, the demands were the calf constantly growing. This is the same as continually adding 10 pounds on your bench press every week. You need to continue to add weight, sleep, and recover to continue to get stronger.

Progressive overload is the most fundamental piece of exercise and of life in general. As you get stronger, whether physically or mentally, you will have to do even more weight/harder things to continue to get stronger. This is easy to think about in terms of school. In most schools, you learn Algebra 1, which is beginner Algebra, before moving on to Algebra 2 or calculus. You need to learn the easier, basic math in order to master the harder, more complex math. This is the same with resistance training; you have to master the lighter weights and easier exercises before progressing on to the heavier weights and more complex exercises. If you've never taken a math class and you sign up for calculus, you will most certainly fail. If you take four years of math in school and gradually work your way up, learning math piece by piece, then by the time you get to college, calculus will be much easier to conquer. This is no different than weight training. Start with the fundamentals, learn the basics, then progress as you grow competence and confidence.

Frequency, Intensity, Time, Type, Volume, and Progression (FITT-VP)

The **FITT-VP model** stands for frequency, intensity, time, type, volume, and progression of exercise. This helps you intelligently and progressively overload your exercises. As you know, you have to continually make your workouts harder in order to continue to improve your fitness. Like Milo, most people think this means you have to increase weight every time you exercise in order to progress. This isn't necessarily the case. Increasing weight (**intensity**) is only one of the many ways you can make a workout harder. If you are only resistance training twice a week, you could add an extra day (increasing **frequency**) and lift three times per week. This is another example

Chapter 1: Principles of Resistance Training (cont.)

of progressive overload. You're making it one day harder, and you will continue to make progress this way. If you squatted 135 pounds for 6 repetitions the first week, by squatting 8 repetitions of 135 pounds the second week, you will also progressive overload via increasing volume. If you usually only do 2 sets of squats at 135 pounds, and you increase it to 3 sets, you will also have increased the volume of the workout and would have succeeded in progressively overloading the muscles. If you usually rest for 3 minutes in between sets of an exercise, but continue doing the same weight and only rest for 2 minutes, you have decreased the amount of **time** in your rest and made that workout harder, meaning you successfully overloaded your muscles. If you add in even more exercises per workout, you have succeeded in progressively overloading those muscles.

As you can see, there are many ways to progressively overload the muscles. You can increase the frequency of your workouts. You can increase the weight on the bar of the exercises. You can decrease the rest in between sets at a given weight. You can also change the **type** of exercise and make it harder. For example, you can switch from a dumbbell bench press to an incline dumbbell bench press, making it harder because your body isn't used to that movement. You can do more sets or more repetitions and increase **volume** (volume is defined as sets x reps x weight). By gradually making things harder over a series of weeks or months, you are progressively overloading your muscles and will continue to improve all areas of physical fitness. The important thing to note is there are many ways to make an exercise program harder using the FITT-VP model. The most important thing is that you make it harder slowly and gradually, only changing one thing at a time. If you change too many things at once or make things too hard right away, you increase the likelihood of getting seriously injured. You must make small and reasonable progressions as you continue to get stronger. More on this will be covered when going over your own workout design later in the book.

Specific Adaptation to Imposed Demands (SAID) Principle

The **SAID principle of specificity** is an acronym that stands for Specific Adaptation to Imposed Demands. Basically, your body adapts to the specific demands you place on it. Let's pretend you want to get better at getting up out of your chair. Well, sitting and standing up is basically just a squat. If you get really good at squatting with weight on your back, then getting out of a chair will become very easy. Let's pretend you want to get better at rock climbing. Well, rock climbing involves a lot of pulling yourself up onto different rocks and ledges. By doing weighted pull-ups and chin-ups, pulling your own body weight up becomes much easier, making rock climbing much easier. Essentially, you train the things you want to get better at in real life. If you want to get faster, you have to strengthen the leg and hip muscles because they're the muscles responsible for running. If you want to get bigger arms, you have to train your biceps, triceps, and shoulders in order to grow bigger arms. You get what you work for.

This is why you have to continue to resistance train as you get older. If you are mostly **sedentary** (sitting a lot) as you work an office job, your body doesn't need muscle mass anymore. You will begin to burn up your muscle mass and begin to store excess fat. Your body turns into whatever your daily habits are and helps you with those daily habits. If you hike every day, you will likely have strong legs and calves because that is what is needed in order to hike every day. If you

Chapter 1: Principles of Resistance Training (cont.)

do heavy manual labor, you will probably be strong all over, because that is what is needed to do heavy manual labor. Your body will adapt to whatever you do every day. This can be a good thing or a bad thing. If you are sedentary, your body will grow soft from the hours of inactivity. With this softness comes obesity, diabetes, cardiovascular disease, and many nervous system diseases. By resistance training, you are adapting your own body to hard work, telling it to build and maintain muscle as you get older. Your muscle holds together your skeleton and is vital at preventing disease and injury. If you want to live an easy life, you must sacrifice a few hours of your work toward resistance training in order to maintain health and wellness and improve physical fitness. If you don't use it, you lose it. In this case, if you don't use your muscle, you will lose it. Luckily, most people don't have to work very physically laborious jobs anymore. Unfortunately, this means we lose a lot of muscle mass just from being sedentary so long. However, weightlifting does a great job at telling our bodies to KEEP and even build, muscle through the SAID principle. This means that you can keep a strong body with only an hour or so of hard work every day instead of 12 like our ancestors.

Energy Systems

A hybrid car has two primary energy systems, electric and gasoline. A hybrid car will use primarily electric energy while at low speeds below 30 miles per hour. Anything faster, and the car will require much faster, more explosive energy and switch to primarily using gasoline as fuel when on the highway. Our bodies are very similar, except we have three energy systems: the creatine phosphate (ATP-PCr) system, the anaerobic lactate (glycolytic) system, and the aerobic (oxygen) system.

The Creatine Phosphate System (ATP-PCr System) is the primary system that provides immediate energy for high-intensity, short duration activities. This energy system provides energy for about the first 10–15 seconds of movement. Hitting a baseball, a high jump, a 40-yard dash, a one rep max, or any activity that is done with full intensity within 10–15 seconds primarily uses the creatine phosphate system. The creatine phosphate system works because the body stores small amounts of **ATP** (adenosine triphosphate) (the body's preferred energy, similar to gasoline) inside of the muscles. ATP is quickly broken down into **ADP** (adenosine diphosphate) and releases energy inside the muscles via a chemical reaction in the process. The creatine phosphate system regenerates ATP from ADP very quickly, but unfortunately runs out of energy very quickly, which is why you immediately run out of gas during a sprint and are forced to slow down. All sprints, heavy weightlifting, jumping, and explosive movements, such as a tennis swing, golf swing, or baseball swing, use the creatine phosphate system. **Creatine** is available in foods such as red meat, seafood, and animal milk. The body also produces creatine in the liver, kidneys, and pancreas. Many athletes supplement creatine, to essentially make sure that this "gas tank" is full and that they can perform to their fullest capabilities during a weightlifting session. Before taking any supplements, you should talk with your doctor or other healthcare professional. This energy system provides the most amount of energy for the highest intensity exercises but also takes the longest to "refill the gas tank" in between sets. It takes between 2–5 minutes of rest after each set of exercise to completely recover before doing another set of high-intensity exercise.

Chapter 1: Principles of Resistance Training (cont.)

The Anaerobic System (Glycolytic System) provides energy for moderate- to high-intensity activities that last about 15 seconds to 2 minutes. At the beginning of any movement, your body primarily uses the creatine phosphate system. Once the body needs more energy than the creatine phosphate system can produce, it switches gears to the anaerobic system, or the glycolytic system. Anytime you hear GLY, you should think sugar, which is stored inside the body as **glycogen** in the muscles. **Glycolytic system** simply means sugar system, meaning your body breaks down

its stored sugar, glycogen, inside the muscles as fuel for the exercise. Carbohydrates break down inside the body and are stored as glycogen before being stored as body fat. This is why people carb load the night before a big game. This fills up your body's glycogen so you can play basketball or soccer at your highest capacity. 400–800 meter sprints, high intensity interval training, or any other sport that requires repeated bursts of activity such as basketball or soccer rely heavily on this energy system. Bodybuilders working out in the higher rep range also rely heavily on this energy system, which is why the timing of carbohydrate ingestion is so important. This can help you make the most out of your weightlifting sessions. This energy system provides energy for the moderate- to high-intensity exercises, and it takes between 2–3 minutes to recover in between each set of exercise.

The Aerobic System (Oxidative System) provides energy for low- to moderate-intensity activities that last longer than 2 minutes. This is the primary energy system for all movement that is low intensity and has to be sustained for a long period of time. Aerobic simply means **oxygen**. This system uses oxygen to convert carbohydrates, fats, and protein into ATP inside the mitochondria of the cells. Long-distance running, cycling, swimming, and all endurance sports primarily use the aerobic system as energy for fuel. The oxygen system does not get used very much during weightlifting activities, so it will be the least important in regard to this book. It is important, however, to maintain a baseline of physical fitness within this energy system. In order to be a well-rounded athlete, the majority of your practices will involve some cardiovascular exercise that will help build up the mitochondria in the body, allowing for more energy to be produced during cardiovascular exercise. This energy system is continuous and does not require very much rest in between sets.

In regard to weightlifting, it is important to know which energy system you are using and for what purpose or sport you are training. For example, football involves short bursts of high-intensity activity. This means your body will primarily use the creatine phosphate and the anaerobic systems during the game. According to the SAID principle, you want to exercise and train the same energy systems you're going to use during your sport. Because weightlifting is a complement to your sport, this means that you will primarily train the creatine phosphate system and the anaerobic system during your weightlifting workouts in order to improve your performance in football. If you are a long-distance runner, you will train all energy systems, but the majority of your weightlifting workouts would be focused around strengthening the aerobic energy system. Not only are you strengthening the muscles in your body when you are weightlifting, but you are also strengthening your energy systems and will improve exercise performance this way as well.

Chapter 1: Principles of Resistance Training (cont.)

This is a chart that will help summarize the energy systems, the repetitions during exercise, the intensity of the exercise, the duration of the exercise, the rest in between sets, and the exercise examples.

Energy System	Rep Range	Intensity	Duration per Set	Rest Period in Between Sets	Example Exercises
Creatine Phosphate System (ATP-PCr)	1–6 Reps	Very High (90–100% 1RM)	0–15 Seconds	3–5 Minutes	Heavy weightlifting, powerlifting, tennis serving, baseball hitting or pitching, explosive track jumps, 40-yard sprint
Anaerobic System (Glycolytic System)	6–12 Reps	Moderate to High (70–85% 1RM)	15–120 Seconds	2–3 Minutes	Moderate weightlifting, bodybuilding, high-intensity interval training, circuit training, CrossFit
Aerobic System (Oxidative System)	15+ Reps	Low to Moderate (50–70% 1RM)	>2 Minutes	Short rest (30–60 seconds) or continuous	Long-distance running, cycling, swimming

It is important to note that exercise intensity is categorized as a percentage of your **1 rep max**. This means the highest amount of weight you can do one time and then calculating your exercise intensity based off of that 1 rep max. So for instance, if you are a football running back, you are mostly concerned with speed, which involves a lot of leg strength. As noted before, football involves very intense short bursts of energy. Following the SAID principle, this athlete will primarily want to strengthen their creatine phosphate system and leg strength, which would involve doing a squat, the most important lower-body exercise for athletes. A coach would first teach the athlete how to squat and then they would test how heavy they can go for one repetition. This would give them their 1 rep max. Let us pretend the athlete can squat 100 pounds for their 1 rep max. In order to strengthen the energy system they will mostly use during the game, the weightlifting coach would assign workouts

Chapter 1: Principles of Resistance Training (cont.)

primarily utilizing the creatine phosphate system with a lot of leg exercises such as the squat. Following the chart, the athlete would work out in the 1–6 rep range doing 90–100 pounds each set of exercise because that is the percentage (90–100%) of their 1RM (100 pounds) that will work that energy system. They will then rest 3–5 minutes before doing another set of squats. If they are working out at the lower percentage, say 90% or 90 pounds, they will probably only need 3 minutes to recover before doing their next set of the exercise. If they are doing the highest percentage, 100% or 100 pounds each set, they will probably need all 5 (if not more) minutes of rest in between each set of exercise before doing another set.

Taking this example and changing the athlete to a track athlete running an 800-meter sprint, which primarily uses the anaerobic, or glycolytic, system, that athlete will primarily work out in the anaerobic exercise zone. This means they will perform 6–12 reps of exercise lifting slightly lighter loads of 70–85% of their one rep max. Because sprinting relies heavily on leg strength, this athlete will also primarily work out the squat. The weightlifting coach would teach the athlete how to squat and find their 1 rep max and base their workouts off of that one rep max. If they also did 100 pounds, then they will primarily exercise between 70–85% of that 1RM in order to strengthen their anaerobic energy system. This means they will squat between 70–85 pounds during their sets of exercise for the bulk of their workout.

As you can see, identify the sport and the needs of the athlete's energy system, find whatever exercise is the closest to the needs of that exercise, test their 1RM, and then you can begin to make the workout based off of their needs. A lineman in football or a shotput athlete will need to focus on the bench press. A gymnast might need to focus on pull-ups or squats. In order to be well rounded, most athletes will use a variety of exercises focusing on movement patterns—pushing, pulling, squatting, hip hinging, and lunging—as these cover all the basic needs of any athlete. Because an athlete will get stronger very quickly, it is important to either retest their 1RM so they can adjust the load of the exercise or to use calculators online to predict a new 1RM periodically. The calculators will ask you how many times you can lift a certain weight and will reliably predict your new 1RM so you don't have to continually test your 1RM. You can save your nervous system the fatigue by using these calculators.

Now that the foundation of energy systems all happening within the body is set, it is important to understand how the body's joints work to perform movement before getting into the exercises.

Chapter 2: Joint Mechanics

Aside from improving performance in sports, the other most important part of weightlifting is reducing the risk of injury during day-to-day activities, sports, and also during your exercise weightlifting training. Weightlifting not only strengthens your muscles, but it also strengthens your bones, tendons, and ligaments. **Wolff's Law** states that bone in a healthy person will adapt to the loads under which it is placed. When you weightlift, you are applying tension to your bones that will tell your body to send signals to the bones to remodel themselves and become stronger over time. **Davis's Law** states that soft tissue structures, such as muscles, tendons, and ligaments, will remodel themselves according to the tension placed on them and become stronger AND more flexible.

Wolff's Law works by regular weightlifting increasing bone density and strength. When lifting weights, especially heavier loads working in the creatine phosphate or anaerobic system, the bones experience stress that stimulates osteoblast activity, leading to the formation of new bone. Over time, the skeletal system adapts to the higher weights when weightlifting and you continually build stronger bones. This prevents osteoporosis and other bone wasting diseases as you age. It also decreases the risk of fractures during exercise and accidents such as car accidents. Since exercises like the squat and deadlift place so much load on the spine, they also make your spine stronger and the bones in your back thicker. This also helps prevent osteoarthritis and degenerative disc disease such as spondylosis.

Davis's Law works by regular weightlifting increasing joint strength and stability. **Tendons** are the soft tissues that attach muscles to bones. **Ligaments** are the soft tissues that attach bones to other bones. These are called **soft tissue** because they are much softer than bones, which are hard and brittle. Most people think that weightlifting only strengthens your muscles, but it also strengthens your tendons and ligaments, making you less likely to injure them during exercise as well. This helps you prevent ACL tears, MCL tears, meniscus tears, and labral tears because all of these things get stronger through regular weightlifting.

Weightlifting correctly will make everything in your body stronger and more flexible. This means many activities in your life will get easier, performance in sports will improve, and you will be less likely to get injured. Your body is a well-oiled machine. Weightlifting trains you to move better in the correct motor patterns that will help prevent injury and also store energy so you can perform to your highest potential, not "leaking" any energy out during movement. In order to move correctly, it is important to understand what each joint does during movement and the primary needs, mobility or stability, of each joint. This will help make weightlifting much safer and help keep the weightlifting athlete from getting injured during weightlifting or participating in sports.

The **joint-by-joint approach** to joint mechanics is a concept that helps you understand the functional movement and stability demands of different joints throughout the body. It states that alternating joints need to be either mobile or stable during movement for the best performance, energy production, and injury prevention. By understanding the needs of the joints, we can also troubleshoot the corrective exercises to fix any joint systems that are faulty. This will prevent injury during weightlifting sessions and prevent injury during sports or real life activities. Most of the corrective exercises can be done during the warmup or cooldown of weightlifting sessions or can be done on rest days so they will not eat up very much of your time. Each joint will be categorized by their primary need (mobility or stability). **Stability** means it has to be strong and stay "in place"

Chapter 2: Joint Mechanics (cont.)

during exercise. **Mobility** means it must be free to move during exercise to prevent injury. All foam rolling exercises should be done for 30–60 seconds and then followed by stretching exercises held for an additional 30–60 seconds.

1. **Foot**
    a. Primary Need: Stability
    b. Type of Joint: Complex structure including tarsal, metatarsal, and phalangeal joints
    c. Corrective Exercise:
        i. Short Foot Exercise: Actively engage the arch by lifting the arch without curling the toes.
    d. Tripod Foot Concept: The tripod foot is the most important concept to understand with regard to the foot during exercise. The foot should be flexed into a short foot position during all leg exercises. This will keep your foot stable during exercise and evenly distribute the weight across all three points of the foot—the heel, base of the big toe, and the base of the little toe. If the foot is stable, it will protect your ankle and knees from injury down the road. If the foot loses stability and your arch collapses, your ankles collapse and your knees cave in or out, increasing the risk of injury to your joints.

2. **Ankle**
    a. Primary Need: Mobility
    b. Type of Joint: Hinge joint
    c. Corrective Exercises:
        i. Ankle Circles: Perform circles with the ankle to enhance range of motion.
        ii. Foam Roll/Massage Gun the Calf
        iii. Calf Stress Against Wall
    d. Mobile Ankle Concept: Stiff ankles are frequently injured ankles or referred to as glass ankles. They are easily rolled, sprained, and strained. When your foot flattens, your ankles cave in and are easily injured. This is why it is important to have a stable foot during exercise. Because the ankle is made up of so many smaller bones, they have the ability to move much more freely, which is why you can move your ankle in many different directions. As long as your ankle maintains its mobility and can move freely, you are much less likely to get injured during movement. Having stiff ankles can result in your heels coming up during squats or other faulty movement patterns. It is important to warmup and stretch the muscles connecting to the ankles in order to keep them loose and not limit ankle mobility by being too tight. The calf and anterior tibialis are the two major muscle groups that connect to the ankle. Keeping them warmed up and loose will help improve ankle mobility.

Chapter 2: Joint Mechanics (cont.)

3. **Knee**
   a. Primary Need: Stability
   b. Type of Joint: Hinge joint
   c. Corrective Exercises:
      i. Squatting with knee stacked on top of ankle and foot
      ii. Lunging with knee stacked on top of ankle and foot
      iii. Single-Leg Balance Exercise
   d. Stable Knee Concept: Your knee is a large hinge joint that is only supposed to extend and flex. If the knee moves sideways, either caving in or caving out, it can damage all of the ligaments that help support the knee, commonly the ACL or MCL. If the ankle is tight and can not move freely, the knee has to make up for its tightness by becoming less stable. This increases the risk of injury and is why we see so many knee injuries. The foot has to be stable in order for the ankle to move freely, and the ankle has to move freely in order for the knee to remain stable during exercise. When performing any leg exercise, the knee should be stacked in a straight line over the ankle and over the foot. This will ensure no energy leaks and will decrease the likelihood of injury during weightlifting and exercise.

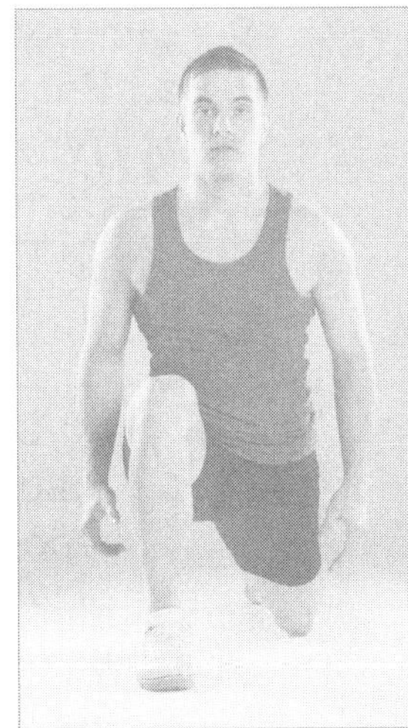

4. **Hip**
   a. Primary Need: Mobility
   b. Type of Joint: Ball-and-socket joint
   c. Corrective Exercises:
      i. Foam roll or massage gun the quads, hamstrings, glutes, and psoas
      ii. Shin Getups
      iii. Hip 90/90
      iv. Hip Flexor Stretch
      v. Hamstring Stretch
      vi. Pigeon Stretch
   d. Mobile Hip Concept: Your hip is a ball-and-socket joint that is designed to be able to move freely in multiple planes of movement. When we sit down too long, our hips are bent and begin to stiffen up. Our hips tend to lose a lot of mobility after sitting in class or at work all day. Because of this, we generally have to focus more time on loosening the hips up when they are feeling tight. If our hips lose mobility, we are forced to borrow mobility from our knees and low back. Because these joints are meant to be stable, our risk of injury goes up. By ensuring our hips stay mobile during exercise, we can help make sure our knees and low back stay stable and decrease the risk of injury during movement.

Chapter 2: Joint Mechanics (cont.)

5. **Lumbar Spine** (Low Back)
    a. Primary Need: Stability
    b. Type of Joint: Multiple intervertebral joints
    c. Corrective Exercises:
        i. Plank
        ii. Side Plank
        iii. Bird Dog
        iv. Dead Bug
    d. Stable Low Back Concept: Low back injuries are some of the most frequently reported injuries in the country. The CDC reported that 28% of men and 31.6% of women aged 18 and older reported LBP (low back pain) in the previous three months. Low back pain with exercise often comes from the low back not being stable enough during exercise. Your core is a cylinder that is filled with air. By practicing the Valsalva maneuver, this pressurized air keeps your low back stable during exercise so that the many spine bones don't become loose and irritate or pinch a nerve. Your low back health and how much you can safely lift depends on how much stability you can produce in your low back. If your low back shifts during exercise, you can get hurt very easily. The majority of core exercises should be exercises that help your body maintain stability in your low back.

6. **Thoracic Spine** (Mid/Upper Back)
    a. Primary Need: Mobility
    b. Type of Joint: Multiple intervertebral joints
    c. Corrective Exercises:
        i. Foam Roll Pecs and Lats
        ii. Lying Thoracic Twists
        iii. Kneeling Thoracic Rotation
        iv. Chest Stretch
        v. Lat Stretch
    d. Mid/Upper Back Concept: Many historians believe our bodies were designed to hang and throw objects. While hanging and throwing objects, our shoulders need a lot of mobility, which involves a lot of rotation of the upper back. We can see this in quarterbacks and baseball/softball players. Swinging motions in sports such as golf, tennis, and baseball/softball also involve a great deal of movement in our upper backs. Our upper backs have to remain mobile in order for our low back to stay stable. Because we oftentimes drive or sit at desks, our upper backs can get rigid, and our posture can get worse over time with a protruding neck. This locks up our upper backs, impairs weightlifting performance, and increases the risk of injury at the low back and neck. Frequent neck pain can be contributed to a lack of mobility in the upper back. Your shoulders and upper back ultimately control where your elbows go during exercise as well. During pushing and pulling exercises, it is crucial that your elbows stay roughly at a 45-degree angle during movement with no more than a 15-degree angle variance. "Elbows locked in" will help ensure the safety of your shoulders during pressing movements.

Chapter 2: Joint Mechanics (cont.)

7. **Elbow**
   a. Primary Need: Stability
   b. Type of Joint: Hinge joint
   c. Corrective Exercises:
      i. Banded Bicep Curls Multidirectional
      ii. Banded Triceps Extensions
      iii. Banded Forearm Flexion/Extension
   d. Elbow Concept: Your elbow is meant to be stable as it helps you stay stable during all pressing and pulling movements. Your elbows have to absorb a lot of force and are meant to stay in place during exercise. Golfer and Tennis Elbow are frequent injuries reported from weak forearm muscles and a lack of upper back mobility. If your elbows lose stability and strength, they can get injured easily. Maintaining strength in your elbows through arm exercises and maintaining a mobile upper back will help your elbows stay healthy during movement.

As you can see, every joint's function alternates continuously between stability and mobility. If the hips are stiff from sitting all day and lose mobility, they have to borrow mobility from the low back and knees, which can result in herniated discs or ACL tears. If the low back is not able to produce very much force, or is weak, then it cannot remain stable on its own and will borrow stability from your upper back or hips, resulting in faulty movement and increased injury.

Foam rolling should be done before your weightlifting session to help ensure that your joints move freely and you stay healthy. It is easy to start at the lower body's calf, then move up to the hamstring and quads, then move to the psoas muscles from your hip to your pelvis, followed by the upper back's lats and pecs. This will greatly enhance range of motion during your exercise and prevent injury. Foam rolling also warms up the tissue by pushing a lot of blood into that area, which also helps prep you for heavy weightlifting. Generally, every session should start with foam rolling.

Foam rolling can be used interchangeably with percussion or vibration therapy equipment such as a massage gun. They essentially do the same thing. You will only want to foam roll one area for 45–60 seconds and then move on, focusing on the areas with the highest tension. Foam rolling can be painful at first, but as your muscles loosen up, it will feel better, and you will immediately have better range of motion affecting those joints. Usually foam rolling is as much as you'll have to do to maintain mobile joints in the areas that need mobility (ankles, hips, and upper back).

Sometimes, however, you will need to do **dynamic mobile exercises**, such as the ankle circles, shin getups, hip 90/90s, thoracic twists, and rotations, if you are still lacking in mobility or have the time to make doubly sure you are prepped for exercise. These exercises help keep your joints mobile and prevent the tissues inside the joints, like your joint capsule, from getting too stiff. You are more likely to have to use these exercises in the middle of winter (when body temperature is lower, muscle tightness will be greater) or before sports that require a great deal of extra mobility, such as gymnastics, jiu-jitsu, or baseball/softball.

Chapter 2: Joint Mechanics (cont.)

If you need more flexibility or mobility than this, you will follow up the dynamic stretches with **static stretch exercises** such as the calf stretch, hamstring stretch, psoas stretch, or wrist stretches. Generally, these are only done in sports where hypermobility is required, such as gymnastics or in physical therapy settings. Most sports do not require static stretching anymore, but if you do feel the need to static stretch, make sure it is done after foam rolling and dynamic stretching is performed so you can get the most out of your static stretch holds. Static stretching can sometimes make you weaker during your weightlifting session, so some weightlifters prefer to wait until after the weightlifting session is completed before static stretching as a part of their cooldown.

By following the joint-by-joint concept and approach to stability and mobility, you can help greatly decrease the risk of injury during your weightlifting sessions. The best way to fix an injury is to never get injured at all, so please take these prehabilitation exercises seriously. More will be discussed in later chapters on the order of performance, but generally every session should start with foam rolling troubled areas and dynamic stretching movements to the joints that need to be mobile during exercise, followed by proper form and body mechanics during the weightlifting session. This helps decrease injury and increase performance and the maximum weight lifted safely during each bout of exercise.

The foot should always be stable, which allows the ankle to stay stacked on the foot, followed by the knee staying in alignment to the ankle and foot. By stacking on top of each other, maximum power can be produced safely within these joints working together.

The low back must remain stable during all movements, which is done by utilizing the **Valsalva maneuver.** This is a breathing technique that stabilizes the core and protects the spine. It involves taking a deep breath and holding in while exerting force around your core muscles contracting around the air. This technique increases intra-abdominal pressure, providing the greatest amount of core and spinal support in the stomach area. It is done as follows:

1. Inhalation:
   a. Before beginning the lift, take a deep breath into the bottom of your stomach filling every bit of your lungs as completely as you can.
   b. This deep inhalation, or breath in, helps expand the chest cavity and diaphragm, allowing the maximum amount of air into your body.

2. Breath-Hold
   a. Hold the breath in and prevent air from escaping by closing your glottis, the part of the throat that controls airflow to the lungs.
   b. This breath-holding creates the pressure within the chest and abdominal cavity that keeps the spine stable and allows energy to flow from the upper body to the lower body, distributing the force of the weight across the body evenly.

3. Execution:
   a. While holding the breath, perform the ENTIRE movement, such as the squat, deadlift, or bench press.
   b. The increased intra-abdominal pressure acts like an internal "brace" that helps stabilize the spine and provides a solid base for the movement.

Chapter 2: Joint Mechanics (cont.)

4. Exhalation:
   a. After the lift is completed, slowly exhale to release the breath. If you are completing another rep of the exercise, restart the process with another inhalation phase and follow the sequence again.

To think simply about the benefits of this technique, imagine a soda can that is filled with pressurized liquid. You can step on a soda can as long as it is sealed and the can will not be crushed easily because of how pressurized the liquid is. If you break the seal and open the can, however, one pound of force will crush the soda can and it will crumble. The soda can is your spine in this analogy, and as long as it's braced, it can withstand hundreds of pounds of pressure, which is why weightlifters can squat and deadlift so much weight without getting hurt. If you are not good at bracing using this technique, however, your spine will crumble like the soda can and you will not be very strong at all.

Benefits:

- Spinal Stability: the increased intra-abdominal pressure from the Valsalva maneuver helps stabilize the spine, reducing the risk of injury to the lower back.
- Enhanced Strength: the stability provided allows for the generation and evenly distributed force of the weight, resulting in improved lifting performance.
- Injury Prevention: the proper use of the maneuver can help prevent injuries by maintaining a rigid torso during heavy lifts.

The most important exercises to be done safely with this maneuver are the squat, deadlift, bench press, and overhead press. These are the most complicated exercises that are the most important because they work every major muscle group in the body and are the foundation of weightlifting exercises.

Application in Key Weightlifting Exercises

- Squat
  - Inhale deeply and brace at the top of the exercise before moving.
  - Maintain breath-hold as you begin to lower and reach the bottom of the exercise.
  - Push up away from the floor to complete the exercise standing completely upright.
  - Exhale after completing the lift.

- Deadlift
  - Take a deep breath and brace around your core before any movement.
  - Remain braced as you push the floor away pulling the barbell from the ground.
  - Keep the breath-hold at the top of the lift and remain holding your breath while you securely sit the barbell back on the ground safely.
  - Exhale once the weight is secure at the floor.

Chapter 2: Joint Mechanics (cont.)

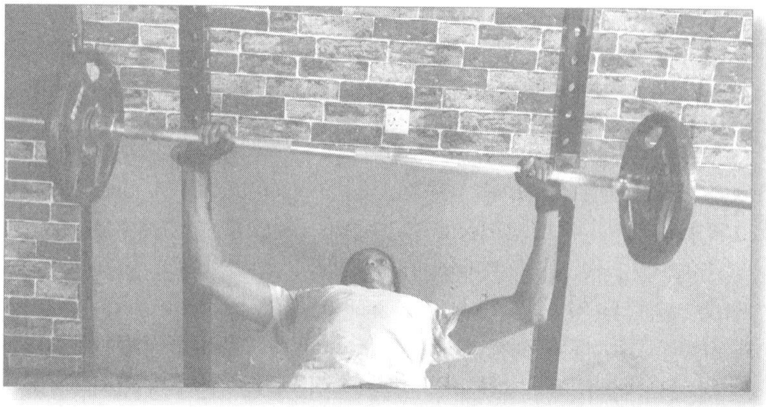

- Bench Press
  - Inhale deeply at the top of the exercise before moving the barbell down to your chest.
  - Remain braced and breath held as you lower the barbell down touching your chest.
  - Tap your chest and begin pushing the bar back up away from your body, all while holding the breath in.
  - Exhale after the barbell is back up into the starting position, fully locked out at the elbows.

- Overhead Press (Military Press)
  - Inhale deeply and brace your core while the barbell is resting at the shoulders in the starting position.
  - Remain braced as you push the barbell up overhead and lock out your elbows at the top of the movement.
  - Keep your breath in as you begin to lower the barbell down back to the starting position at your shoulders.
  - Exhale once the bar is back safely into the starting position resting on your shoulders.

As you can see, each and every rep of every major exercise should be done utilizing the Valsalva maneuver to keep your core and low back safe during exercise. Every rep will need to be braced and rebraced after the rep is completed. Common mistakes include breathing out or releasing your brace as you're doing the lift. This is a mistake because you never want your spine to lose rigidity while you're performing an exercise. You only want to exhale once the lift is totally completed. If you have more repetitions to complete your set, you must repeat the cycle of inhaling and bracing for each and every rep. This will help keep every rep as safe as possible and prevent injury. This might make it harder to breathe on the higher rep sets, but this will only increase your lung capacity and endurance during exercises. Maintaining safety during exercise is the most important part of any weightlifting session.

Chapter 3: Movement Pattern-Based Weightlifting

Weightlifting has changed significantly across the decades. From bodybuilding to Olympic weightlifting to strongman competitions, all weightlifting is defined as the use of resistance, in many cases weights, in specific exercises as a part of a strength training program designed to improve muscle mass, strength, and overall physical fitness. This can be done using **isolation exercises** that target specific muscles, such as calf raises to make the calf bigger and stronger, or by compound exercises we will term as movement pattern-based exercises, which are the primary focus of this book. **Movement pattern-based weightlifting** focuses on training the body through fundamental movement patterns rather than isolating specific muscles. Everybody on earth has a subset of movement patterns that they use every single day, similar to computer programs your computer runs every day. These movement patterns work multiple muscle groups at a time in order to move weight, which is why they are commonly called **compound exercises**.

Seven Movement Patterns

Your body has seven total movement patterns that we will break down in this book: squat, hip hinge, lunge, push, pull, twist/rotation, and carry. Every movement you do throughout the day involves a combination of these seven movements. By primarily focusing on weightlifting exercises that involve all seven of these movements, you will improve your overall functional fitness, strength, and coordination, build muscle, burn body fat, and reduce the risk of injury by promoting a balanced development and proper movement mechanics. Generally, the more muscles you work throughout a workout, the more growth and the more athletic you will become.

Squat

The **squat** is a lower-body movement where the hips, knees, and ankles flex to lower the body and then extend to raise it back up. The squat directly strengthens the quadriceps, hamstrings, glutes, and core. The squat is the single greatest exercise for building lower-body strength, balance, coordination, and speed. Every time you squat down to a seat, you are practicing a squatting movement pattern.

Hip Hinge

The **hip hinge** is a lower-body movement primarily involving the hips where the torso bends forward at the hips while maintaining a neutral spine. The hip hinge can be thought of as a deadlift movement and strengthens the entire posterior chain, including the hamstrings, glutes, low back, and core. The **hip extension** is the same as the hip hinge, except lying down instead of standing up, so it can be thought of as a glute bridge or hip thrust motion. The hip hinge exercises build the most strength in picking up objects, which has a huge carryover to everyday life and work. Every time you bend over to pick something up off the floor, you are practicing a hip hinge movement pattern.

Chapter 3: Movement Pattern-Based Weightlifting (cont.)

Lunge

The **lunge** is a single-leg movement involving stepping forward, backward, or to the side and lowering the hips. A **step up** is categorized beneath the lunge, the only difference being your hips raise as you climb up the step, versus your hips lower as you get closer to the ground with a lunge. Both the lunge and step up strengthen the quadriceps, hamstrings, glutes, and core. They also greatly improve balance and coordination, especially standing on one leg. Every time you walk up or down a set of stairs, you are using a step up movement pattern and every time you are lunging down to tie your shoes, you are using a lunge movement pattern.

Push

The **push** will be further categorized into horizontal pushing exercises and vertical pushing exercises. A push is an upper-body movement where the arms extend away from the body. All pushing exercises strengthen the chest, shoulders, and triceps. If you've ever pushed furniture or a fridge across the room or even pushed a shopping cart, you have practiced a pushing movement pattern in your day-to-day life.

Pull

The **pull** is an upper-body movement where the arms pull toward the body. The pull will be further categorized into horizontal pulling exercises and vertical pulling exercises. Pulling exercises strengthen the back, biceps, and forearms. If you've ever had to do a pull up in class or played tug of war for fun, you have practiced a pull-up movement pattern. Even pulling open heavy doors into stores is a great example of why it's important to train your pulling movements!

Twist/Rotation

A **twist/rotation** is a movement that involves rotating the torso. It enhances core strength, stability, and rotational power, which is crucial for most competitive skill-based sports. Turning your back to look behind you, putting on your seatbelt, golfing, swinging a baseball bat, and playing tennis are all examples of core-twisting/rotation movement patterns that occur either in sport or leisure settings.

Chapter 3: Movement Pattern-Based Weightlifting (cont.)

Carry

A **carry** involves holding weight while moving, focusing on stability and endurance. This movement improves grip strength, core stability, and total body endurance. This is frequently referred to as farm strength. If you've ever had to carry a 5-gallon bucket of grain, water, or just a ton of groceries in your hands, you have practiced a carry movement pattern.

There are many benefits of movement pattern-based weightlifting. As you can see, there are many examples of how you use these movement patterns in normal day-to-day life. You also use them in all sporting activities, whether they are competitive or recreational. It is therefore important to train each and every movement pattern in order to stay a well-rounded, healthy human. You can expect functional strength increases, which will enhance the ability to perform daily activities and sports with better efficiency and less risk of injury. You will also gain better balance in muscular development and address potential weaknesses or imbalances within the body. Keeping muscle imbalances to a minimum will help you stay healthy, apply an equal load on your spine, and avoid overuse injuries. By training movements rather than isolating muscles like bodybuilders, you will become more resilient and train specifically for how you will carry out real life functions, making you less likely to get injured every day. You will improve neuromuscular coordination and movement quality, which is your brain's way of talking to your muscles. This decreases your risk of Alzheimer's disease and dementia and other brain-muscle diseases as you age.

Lastly, because every movement works so many different muscles, you will save a lot of time in the gym by doing less exercises but working out more muscles. Bodybuilders who specifically isolate each and every muscle group have to do 3–5 exercises *per muscle group* each bout of exercise. This means that if they are working their upper body, they will have to train their chest, triceps, shoulders, biceps, and back all separately, resulting in 15–20 exercises per workout. They could do more compound exercises like the pushing exercises, which work three different muscle groups at once, saving hours of exercise per week. You can simply get more done and grow faster and stronger in less time by focusing on compound movement pattern-based weightlifting. That is not to say isolation exercises don't serve a purpose in rehabilitation settings or professional bodybuilding. They should just be used sparingly and in certain circumstances.

Overall, no exercise is bad exercise, but compound movement pattern-based weightlifting takes up a lot less time and reaps a larger number of benefits, and therefore will be the primary focus of this book. The next chapters will break down the movements from easiest exercise to learn to the hardest exercises to learn. It is always better to start with easier movements and learn them before progressing to the harder, more risky movements. Master the easy movements in order to make mastering the harder movements easier.

Chapter 4: Squat

Squat

Every single time you sit down and get up from a chair, you are essentially performing a **squat**. This is the most foundational movement pattern for lower-body movement. The squat is fundamental for daily life in your ability to perform day-to-day tasks as well as any recreational or sporting activity. Getting better at squatting improves your ability to walk, jog, run, sprint, stand up, hop, jump, skip, lunge, step up, or any other activity that involves using your legs. It is the easiest leg exercise to learn because it takes the least amount of low back strength (like a hip hinge) and the least amount of coordination to learn (like a lunge or step up). Therefore, it is the first lower-body exercise someone should learn and master before progressing to any other movement because it has such a big carry over into other movements.

Squatting works a ton of major muscle groups in your core and your legs. This will make all of the bones in your spine and lower body thicker and stronger, avoiding fractures, osteopenia, and osteoporosis. It will also make your muscles, tendons, and ligaments more flexible and stronger as well, avoiding soft tissue injuries in the knees, ankles, hips, and low back. Squatting also builds a large amount of muscle. This is called muscle **hypertrophy**, or larger muscles. The bigger your muscles are, the more sugar or carbohydrates they can store as glycogen. This improves your insulin response and helps prevent type 2 diabetes. Because the legs are so vascular and squatting is so demanding, a good squat workout will also work your circulatory system, giving your heart a workout and helping prevent heart disease. Squatting will help prevent both acute and chronic diseases and help you age better and healthier.

The squat works your **quadriceps** (the front of the thighs), which are your muscles responsible for extending the knee during the upward portion of the squat. They also aid in stability in your knee and play a large role in prevention of injuries involving the knee.

The squat also works your **gluteus maximus** (your butt muscle), which is the primary muscle for hip extension and helps in standing up from the squatting position. Your glutes are like the base of the pyramid that your low back sits on. If you have weak glutes, you will have a weak low back. Your glutes also stabilize your hip joint, which helps prevent injuries to the hips.

The squat works your **hamstrings** (back of the thighs) as it primarily provides stability for the knee joint in assisting hip extension. Your hamstrings help stabilize your hip and your knee during movement. This helps prevent hamstring tears in sports like soccer and football.

The squat works your **adductors** (inner thighs), as well as stabilizing your groin and legs during the squat, stretching out your hips in the bottom of the squat. This helps tone the inner portion of your thigh as well as prevents groin tears and strains during sprinting or lateral side-to-side movement.

Chapter 4: Squat (cont.)

The squat works your **erector spinae** (lower back) by maintaining a semi-upright position and provides spinal stability during the movement when paired with the Valsalva maneuver. This leg exercise does not involve your back as much as a hip hinge or deadlift does, but it will help make it significantly stronger so you can progress to hip hinges safely without worrying about injuring your low back.

The squat also works all of your **core muscles**, providing stability and support around your braced air, supporting your spine and pelvis throughout the movement. Because the squat is generally placing the load on your spine, your core has to prevent your spine from compressing during movement. This means your core will get significantly stronger the stronger your squats get.

Finally, the squat also helps the **hip flexors**, which are the muscles primarily used during sprinting, by maintaining balance and stability during the lowering phase of the squat.

As you can see, the squat is very important and hosts a variety of benefits for the entire body. The hard part is usually getting started with the exercise. Luckily, regardless of the type of squat that you are doing, the same basic rules are used for every single type of squat. When learning to squat, it is best to start with the easiest variation to learn the basic rules, and then move on to the next progression of squat once the fundamentals are learned at each stage of the exercise. Exercise progressions of the squat consist of: goblet box squat, goblet squat, barbell box squat, front squat, and finally, the barbell back squat.

Squatting Rules

After mastering the joint-by-joint approach, the rules of mastering the squat are much easier to learn. When performing any exercise, we will start visualizing the process from the ground up. First, you must make your foot stable. You do this by performing the short foot and digging your feet into the ground. Pretend to grab the floor with your feet as if you have talons. This creates stability in your foot, which allows your ankle to travel freely. Next, drive your knees out so they travel in line with your toes. The cue to think about with this is "open hips" while you're squatting. When looking in a mirror, your knees should be traveling perpendicular, stacked right on top of your ankles and feet. They should not be caving in; that is a common lifting fault called **valgus knee** and will increase the risk of injury if repeatedly exercised. You want your feet solid, your ankles stacked right on top of your feet, and your knees stacked on top of your ankles. For squatting, your toes can be pointed slightly out anywhere from 10 degrees to 30 degrees. If you are stiff or have wide hips, it will be easier to squat turning your toes out. Regardless of toe angle, your knees must be stacked on top of your feet and in line with the direction of your feet. The more you have your toes pointed out, the more you will have to drive your knees out. It is recommended to turn them out as little as possible, but due to hip anatomy, everyone's squat will look slightly different. Most importantly, find what is most comfortable for you that allows your foot, ankle, and knee to be stacked on top of each other. This will allow the greatest ankle mobility, knee stability, and hip mobility to lessen the risk of injury. If

Knee Angle During Squat

Chapter 4: Squat (cont.)

your feet collapse, your knees will cave in. Make sure your feet stay stable and you drive your knees out. Generally, your knees should be slightly wider than your hips when beginning the movement. If your legs are too wide, it will be impossible to stack your feet, ankles, and knees on top of each other. If they are too narrow, your knees will go too far out and you will fall.

As mentioned before, the **Valsalva maneuver** will be used before any movement. You will breathe into your low stomach and brace your core against the braced air. Next, you will always move your hips back, or hip hinge, before ever bending your knees. With squatting, you will move your hips back very slightly and then bend your knees. A common mistake is bending the knees first—this will place more strain on your low back trying to stay too far upright. Always initiate the movement with your hips before bending your knees. This will make sure the load is placed on your glutes and hamstrings. Then bend the knees, transferring the load to the quadriceps. You will then move downward, bending the knees until you reach the bottom of the exercise, and then squat back up. You will maintain that brace while you decend and ascend back up, completing the lift and breathing again for another repetition. Whether you are sitting on a bench or doing a total squat, these rules will be your guide for learning every squat progression. Whenever possible, squat in front of a mirror so you can visually check up and down your body to make sure your form is correct on each and every repetition.

Goblet Box Squat

The **goblet box squat** is the easiest and therefore the first squat progression you will have to master to become an expert squatter. In order to learn the rules for squatting, it is easiest to learn while sitting down on a box or bench. This limits your range of motion so there's less risk of falling or getting hurt squatting down too far. By holding the weight in front of you, you can maintain a more upright position and feel your core muscles stabilize better, making it the best exercise to learn the fundamentals of the squat. You will find a bench or a box that allows you to sit down to parallel, and your hip crease should be even or below your knee crease at the bottom of the squat. The lower you go, the more range of motion of the hips and quadriceps and the harder the exercise will be. We recommend learning the movement by only box squatting to parallel until the lift is mastered, and then you can lower the bench height to sit deeper in the squat. Following the rules of the squat, you will pause at the bottom once you've sat down completely, rock back slightly, rock forward slightly, and squat up. When you sit down, you want to maintain as much tension on your muscles as possible, trying to only sit down with 50% of your bodyweight. Do not breathe out at the bottom. Make sure your breath is braced throughout the entire lift.

Goblet Box Squat

Chapter 4: Squat (cont.)

Goblet Squat

The **goblet squat** is a continuation of the goblet box squat. You are removing the safety net of the bench. You will be able to squat deeper with better range of motion. The more range of motion, the healthier your joints will be, and the more muscle and strength you will build. This is called **stretch mediated hypertrophy**. When learning to goblet squat, you might only be able to go parallel at first. Once you've mastered this, we suggest going slightly below parallel. This will help improve hip mobility and flexibility and strengthen your thighs more. Be careful not to squat so deeply that you lose your upright torso position and round your back. You only want to squat as deeply as you can maintain a flat lower back. Unlike the goblet box squat, do not pause at the bottom of the squat. Simply grab the floor with your feet, breathe, brace your core, move your hips back, drive your hips open, bend your knees, go down until you've reached your bottom position, and then stand back up. Once you've mastered the goblet squat, you can master any squat variation. Double check that your knees, ankles, and feet are stacked on top of each other.

Goblet Squat

Barbell Box Squat

The **barbell box squat** is the first squat progression that will utilize a weight on your back instead of in front of you with a dumbbell. The reason you must graduate from goblet squats with a dumbbell to a back squat is because your legs will simply get too strong too quickly for your hands to be able to hold a dumbbell that heavy. For someone learning to squat, they can easily work up to a 200-pound back squat in under two years of training. A dumbbell that heavy would be impossible to hold in front of you. If you don't move on to mastering the barbell, your legs will not get any stronger or grow any muscle mass. I know it can be intimidating learning to use a barbell for the first time, but if you've mastered the goblet squat variations, I'm confident you can master the barbell variations.

Knowing where to place the barbell can be tricky. You can set the bar on your upper trap muscles, which is called a **high bar position**, which is usually easier and more comfortable to learn. You can also place the bar on your shoulder blades, slightly lower than the traps, in a position called a **low**

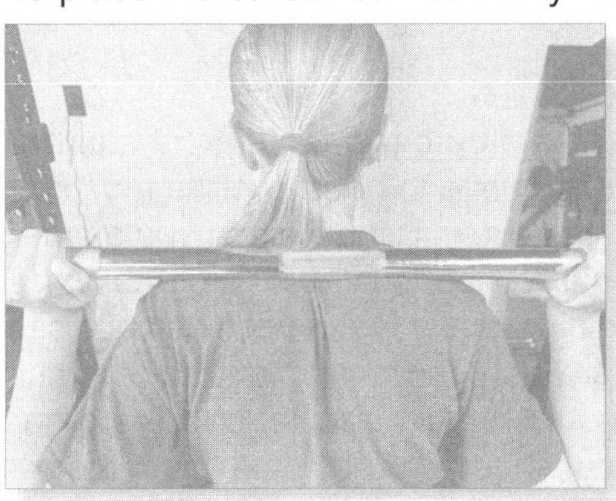

High Bar Position

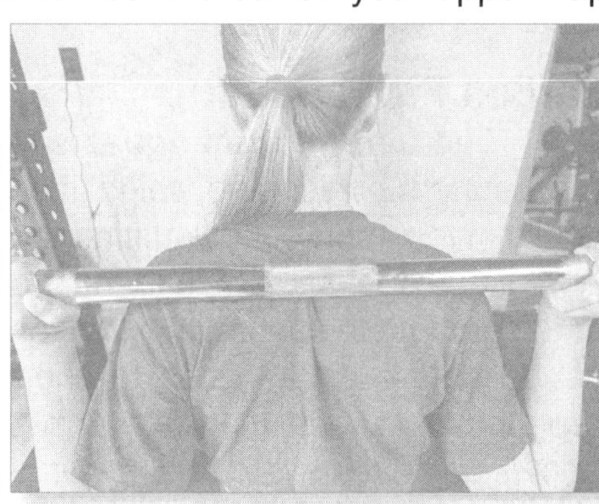

Low Bar Position

Chapter 4: Squat (cont.)

bar position. The higher the barbell, the more upright your torso will be and the more quadriceps (front thigh) you will work. The lower the barbell, the more glutes you will work when squatting. If your goal is to grow your thighs, train high bar squats first. If your goal is to grow your butt muscles, train low bar squats. Generally, jumping athletes will train front squat or high bar squat because jumping requires the most strength at the knees, or quadriceps. Sprinting athletes will want to master the low bar squat because sprinting requires a lot of strength from the hips.

Do not use a pad when squatting. It might feel comfortable at first, but you need to be able to feel the weight on your back and stack your upper back tightly against the bar in order to progress in weight appropriately. Using a pad shuts off your upper back muscles and will make you more likely to get injured during the exercise.

Barbell Box Squat

Once you've practiced the position on your back, the barbell box squat is almost identical to the goblet box squat. You will line up your hands on the bar. You will slip under the bar and place it either in the high bar or low bar position. Low bar requires more shoulder mobility, so if you have to foam roll your pecs and lats or work on your upper-body mobility, do so before your squatting session. Move your hands as close to the midline of your body as possible, which will keep your upper back and spine tighter and reduce the risk of injury. Stand directly up with the bar placed soundly on your back. Walk two steps back with the bench directly behind you. You will grab the floor with your feet using the short foot method and then you will brace your spine by breathing in and incorporating the Valsalva maneuver. Move your hips back to initiate the movement and then begin to bend your knees. Once you've reached the box, sit 50% of your weight on the bench, slightly rocking back. Rock forward, stand up, and exhale once the rep is completed. Rebrace and repeat if you are continuing your set.

Barbell Front Squat

The **barbell front squat** is the next progression. The front squat position allows for more of an upright position so weightlifters don't have to bend over as much. The front squat is also a key lift in the sport of powerlifting and CrossFit, utilizing a clean grip on the bar. Movement will feel more like a goblet squat than the previous low bar box squat progression. This will allow for you to sit deeper into the squat and work on your range of motion and balance similar to the goblet squat. Hands should be as close to shoulders as possible (potentially slightly wider than shoulders, depending on wrist mobility). Arms should remain parallel with the ground, trying to keep your elbows pointed forward and up. Only your fingertips should be under the bar. Mastering this motion will allow you to master the clean and jerk and the power snatch exercises if you want to progress

Chapter 4: Squat (cont.)

to Olympic lifts. These are common lifts Olympic lifters or athletes in college will use, but are beyond the scope of this book because they take a long time to learn and master, as they are much more complicated than traditional movement pattern-based training. It is best to master the front squat before ever attempting a clean, jerk, or snatch exercise.

Barbell Front Squat

Similarly to the other squat variations, you will grab the floor with your feet. The bar will be placed in front of you and rest on your delt muscles by the space next to your collar bone. Elbows will remain pointed forward and up during the motion. This will force your torso to stay very upright as opposed to a back squat. This will be very difficult for some people to get into position, so it will take some getting used to in order to master this exercise. If you are not planning to compete in CrossFit or play college sports, you can probably skip the front squat and move directly into a full back squat.

Barbell Back Squat

Barbell Back Squat

The **barbell back squat** is the king of all squatting exercises. Removing the bench, you will be able to sit at parallel or below parallel depending on your mobility. Strength training competitions only require you to sit to parallel, but I recommend training slightly below parallel for knee and hip health. You will get under the bar and use the same position you learned in the barbell box squat. The set up is exactly the same. When you walk out, you will just take several small steps back. Next, you will grab the floor with your feet using the **short foot method**. You will keep your back tight, imagining you are bending the bar into your back, pulling the bar into you. This will help maintain maximum rigidity in your thoracic spine. Breathe in and brace your core. Once braced, move your hips back to initiate the movement. You will then bend your knees and sit down as low as you can without rounding your back, and then proceed to stand back up. If you took the time to master the previous exercises, this will feel incredibly easy and you will be fully prepared to load up the weight.

Chapter 4: Squat (cont.)

The same rules as the other squats apply to the back squat, except with the back squat, you can go much heavier than all the other squat variations. This means you should take extra care to warm up and progress slowly.

Transformer Bar

The **transformer bar** is an amazing new tool for squatting that combines a safety squat bar and takes it to the next level. As previously mentioned, when the load is further in front of you like in a goblet squat, front squat, or high bar position, you will work more of your quadriceps muscles and maintain a more upright position. This is great for jumping athletes or people who want to build the most amount of quad muscle they can. If you're a sprinting athlete, volleyball player, or simply want to grow your glutes, you will want to master the low bar squatting position because the weight is further behind you. The transformer bar allows you to set the weight either in front of you or behind you in every type of squatting movement pattern, all while having the comfort of a pad and handles so you do not have to worry about hand placement. Learn how to use a traditional barbell first because most gyms are not fortunate to have a bar like this and no power lifting, CrossFit, or Olympic lifting sports will allow you to use this type of barbell. For average gym-goers, this is a great bar with a lot of capabilities to work different leverages and muscle groups.

Failing a Lift

Chances are you will fail a squat some day. Always use clips when squatting to prevent the weights from shifting and falling off the bar. You should always have a spotter standing behind you, ready to catch you and help you back up if you fail a lift. If you are going heavy enough, you might even need three spotters: one behind you and one on either side of you to help you stand back up and rerack the weight. If you do not have a spotter, however, and still plan to squat, you should practice failing the squat. You will need to let go of the bar, getting your hands out of the way, and very quickly walk forward. The bar will fall behind you and make a lot of noise as it either hits the ground or the safety bars catch the barbell and weight. This will be embarrassing, but it is better to be embarrassed than die or suffer a severe neck injury from letting the bar fall on top of your neck. Always use clips, always use a spotter, and always make sure the safety arms are at an appropriate height (so when you sit down at the bottom of your squat, the safety arms should be close, but not touching the barbell at the bottom of your movement), to minimize the risk of something bad happening if you fail a lift. Worst case scenario, drop the weight BEHIND you and sprint forward.

Chapter 4: Squat (cont.)

Activity

On a large notecard, copy this set of squat cues so you have an easy-to-follow checklist to bring with you to the gym to make sure you're squatting correctly.

Squat Setup and Form

Stance:	Position your feet slightly wider than shoulder width apart. Your toes should be between 10–30 degrees pointed out.
Bar Position:	High Bar: Position the barbell on your upper trap shelf. Avoid setting the bar right on your neck.
	Low Bar: Position the barbell on your rear deltoids, just below the trap muscle.
Grip:	Place your hands on the bar just outside your shoulders. Your grip should be firm with your wrists as straight as can be and your elbows pointing down, pulling the barbell into your back.
Body Position:	Keep your spine neutral, bracing and engaging your core to maintain this position.
Chest and Shoulders:	Keep your chest up as you're going down and coming up. If you let your chest down, you will fall forward.
Neck:	Look five feet in front of you slightly down. For many, they will be squatting up against the wall. Look at where the wall meets the floor. DO NOT look up, as you will increase the likelihood of straining your neck.

Key Cues for Squatting

Grip the Floor With Your Feet:	Using the short foot, grip the floor with your feet as if you had talons and are gripping the floor. Maintain an equal three points of contact (your big toe, little toe, and heel) throughout the lift.
Breathe and Brace:	Take a deep breath into the bottom of your stomach and brace your core around the air. Maintain tightness and hold your breath throughout the entire lift.
Hips Back and Down:	Always initiate the movement by pushing your hips back and then bending the knees.
Knees Over Toes:	Open your hips and drive your knees out so your knees track over in line with your ankles and feet. Do not let the knees cave in during any part of the movement.
Depth:	Lower yourself down until your hip crease is below your knees. Do not go so low that your low back rounds; only go as low as your low back will allow you to.
Stand Up:	As you rise, drive through your entire foot, pushing your knees out slightly. Keep your chest up. You should stand up evenly.
Breathe Out and Reset:	As you complete the lift, breathe out while still maintaining some tension in your core to keep you stable. Rebreathe and rebrace before continuing on with your next rep.

Chapter 5: Hip Hinge/Hip Extension

Hip Hinge/Hip Extension

Every time you bend over to pick something up off the ground or do any sort of bridging motion, like in wrestling, you are essentially doing a hip hinge/hip extension movement. In fact, every squat begins with a hip hinge, pushing the hips back, then bending the knees. Hip extensions primarily focus on pushing the hips back with a slight bend of the knees. Whatever joint gets the most range of motion gets worked the most, which is why this movement is called a hip hinge or extension. Hinging the hips back and then extending the hips forward where they get the majority of the work done is called a **hip hinge** or a **hip extension**. The hip hinge plays off of the squat so it is important to master the squat before moving into the hip hinge. The hip hinge will help you lift heavy items off the ground without injuring yourself. It will help you get better at sweeping and vacuuming, picking up boxes, gardening, and moving planters—essentially every daily task that involves bending over or moving at the hips. With athletic activities, it will help you jump higher, sprint faster, become more explosive in your starting positions in tennis or volleyball, and all around make you a better athlete.

Because the hip hinge/hip extension motion strengthens so many muscle groups in your core and your legs, they help prevent all the same diseases the squat motion does. Diseases such as cardiovascular disease, type 2 diabetes, stroke, osteoporosis, and sarcopenia can be improved and prevented in some cases through resistance training these movement patterns. The hip hinge especially requires a large amount of nervous system recruitment, which helps prevent and manage neurodegenerative diseases. Your bones and soft tissue (muscles, tendons, and ligaments) will also get significantly stronger, helping to avoid acute injuries as well.

The hip hinge/hip extension movement pattern works your **hamstrings** (back of the thigh) through being the primary mover in hip extension. This helps your body decelerate when running, sprinting, and jumping, subsequently improving your speed, slow down, agility, and pivot time, and making you less likely to injure your hamstring during sports.

The hip hinge/hip extension also works your **gluteus maximus** (butt muscle) as a primary mover in hip extension. This makes your hips stronger, which lays the foundation for your low back. The stronger your hips, the stronger and more stable your low back will be during movement. This also helps generate key power to help athletes jump and sprint.

The hip hinge/hip extension also significantly utilizes the **erector spinae** (low back) to maintain spinal alignment and stability lifting heavy loads. This helps strengthen your low back and avoid osteoarthritis and degenerative disc disease in the spine.

The hip hinge/hip extension stabilizes the **trunk and pelvis** during movement, helping you stay aligned and sprint and run faster during exercise.

As you can see, the hip hinge/hip extension will be very useful in your training to develop speed, power, strength, muscle size, coordination, and stability, and decrease the likelihood of injury during sports and day-to-day life. It is an otherwise fundamental life skill that must be practiced in order to be perfected. As with the squat, it is easiest to learn the most basic form of hip hinge/hip extension before progressing to the next variation. Because they are two slightly

Chapter 5: Hip Hinge/Hip Extension (cont.)

different movements, we will alternate movements so you can master two at a time. Kettlebell deadlift, barbell glute bridge, trap bar deadlift, deficit trap bar deadlift, barbell hip thrust, and finally the conventional barbell deadlift will be your movements to master, in that order, to make sure you have the easiest and safest time learning the exercises.

Hip Hinge/Deadlift Rules

All lower-body exercises share some common themes like grab the floor with your feet, drive knees out so they're traveling in line with your toes, open your hips, brace your core using the Valsalva maneuver prior to beginning the exercise, and always initiate the exercise with a hip hinge. At this time, you should have mastered the squat, so the **deadlift** will be much easier to learn. All of these same rules apply with only a few differences. Instead of the bar being placed on your back, you are picking the bar up from the ground, standing up, and then slowly lowering it down, controlling the weight all the way back down. All deadlifts are just different variations of hip hinges, so those words will be used interchangeably.

With the deadlift, your stance will be closer than with the squat. Your feet should be about hip width apart. You should walk up to the bar so that the barbell is right over your midfoot. The farther out the bar, the more strain on your low back, so keeping it close to your body is a must. You will then push the hips back and bend over to grab the bar. When learning the movement, use a double overhand grip. As the weight gets heavier, you will have to add chalk or liquid chalk to increase the friction to hold on to heavier weights. Once you no longer can hang on to the bar or you start to lose your grip, you will need to either invest in weightlifting straps, or if you plan on lifting for grip strength or sports, use a mixed grip with one hand over and one hand under as pictured in the deadlift. You want to grab the bar right outside of your knees. Your arms should almost touch your knees in the starting position. Your feet should grab the ground like talons, and you should open your hips up so your knees are stacked on top of your ankles and feet to avoid muscle imbalances and injuries. Your hips should be pushed back as if you were reaching behind you. Your spine should be neutral/flat and avoid any lifting with a round back. You will want to tuck your shoulder blades back, imagining you are squeezing oranges down in between your arm pits. This will ensure your back stays flat throughout the lift. Now you are set up to do a deadlift.

Kettlebell Deadlift

The **kettlebell deadlift** is the easiest variation of the deadlift and only requires a kettlebell to perform. Following the hip hinge rules, you will walk up to the kettlebell and imagine the handle is the barbell. The kettlebell will be between your feet and the handle will cut an imaginary line through the middle of your foot when looking down. The farther an object is away from your feet, the farther you will have to pull it, and the more load will be placed on your low back. You can practice if you want; this will show you how important it is to keep the deadlift/kettlebell as close to your body as possible when lifting it. In fact, you will want to keep any and all objects you lift from the ground as close to your body as possible, which will make the movement easier and help you avoid injury. Your legs will be hip-width apart, which is a little closer than a goblet squat would be. Your toes should be pointing either straight forward or up to a 30-degree angle out. If your toes naturally turn in, you will want to point them straight ahead. If your feet naturally turn out, go in line with how they are naturally oriented. The most important part is that your knees stay stacked over your feet and ankles in alignment and do not cave in.

Chapter 5: Hip Hinge/Hip Extension (cont.)

Once your feet are set, push your hips back to bend over and place your hands on the kettlebell handle. Your hips will be pushed back much farther than a squat and your knees will be bent slightly. You will then tuck your armpits down as if you were squeezing an orange between them. This will help ensure your back stays flat throughout the movement. If your back rounds, you are much more likely to get injured and suffer a back strain. Do not lift with a rounded back if you can help it.

Kettlebell Deadlift

Take a deep breath into your stomach and brace around the air. Once braced, push the floor away from you in a squatting motion until the kettlebell reaches your knees, then drive your hips forward to complete the lift. Squeeze your glutes hard together to lock out the lift. Once it is locked out, initiate the descent, or moving down, phase by pushing your hips back. Always lead with the hips. Once the kettlebell reaches your knees, bend your knees down and squat the rest of the way down. Once the kettlebell is safely back on the ground, breathe out and reset your breath for the next repetition.

Barbell Glute Bridge

The glute bridge is one of the oldest hip extension exercises. For decades, it has been used in physical therapy settings for knee pain, hip pain, and low back pain. The glute bridge primarily strengthens and focuses on the gluteus maximum (hips/butt), hamstrings (back of the thigh), and low back. The barbell glute bridge is just an easier way to overload the muscles to make them even stronger. The glute bridge focuses on the extension of the hip by activating and strengthening the glutes. With strong glutes, walking, running, jumping, and squatting will be that much easier. It will also help iron proof your low back so you can handle heavier loads during your squats and deadlifts. For increased athletic performance, making everyday activities easier, and building up glute strength and size, the hip extension exercises, starting with the barbell glute bridge, are the best exercises for glute-specific size and strength gains.

To set up the barbell glute bridge, you will want to use bumper plates so that the height of the bar is high enough you can roll over your legs. **Bumper plates** are rubber training plates that come in 5-, 10-, 15-, 25-, 35-, and 45-pound increments. The rubber plates are all the same height as a 45-pound iron plate. This is the same for hip thrusts. If you are a small teen, you could probably use 25- or 35-pound regular iron plates and roll

Barbell Glute Bridge Starting Position

Chapter 5: Hip Hinge/Hip Extension (cont.)

Barbell Glute Bridge

them over your legs. You will want to definitely make sure to have a squat pad/cushion over the barbell so it can rest on your hip bones and protect your hips. After making sure the height can be rolled over your legs, you will lie down on the ground. Roll the barbell over your legs and onto your hip bones with the pad centered safely on the hips. You will bring your legs in so that your heels are almost touching your butt. When you are at the top of the rep, your knees should be at a 90-degree angle. Too far forward and you will mostly feel your hamstrings doing the work. If this is the case, you will need to move your feet closer to your butt to work your hips more. If they are too close, your heels will come off the ground. If this happens, move your feet farther out so that your feet can remain planted and grabbed to the floor. Grip the bar with an overhand grip wider than shoulder width apart, fully extending your arms while pushing against the bar so that the bar does not roll down onto you during the lift.

Engage your core by breathing into your stomach and bracing your core around the air. You will press through your mid foot/heel into the ground, driving your hips up toward the ceiling. This will lift the barbell off the ground. Make sure to push the barbell away from your body so that it does not roll down. Squeeze your glutes at the top for one second to fully engage them. Slowly lower the weight back down, bringing your hips back toward the ground in a controlled manner. You will then breathe out and breathe back in, resetting your core before repeating another rep. To make the glute bridge harder, instead of adding weight, you can add seconds to the pause at the top of the lift. By squeezing your glutes for three seconds of a pause at the top, you will drastically increase glute activation and strength. This will save you time from having to add more weight onto the bar each week; you can simply add a longer pause to make this exercise more difficult.

Trap Bar Deadlift

The **trap bar**, or **hex bar**, is an awesome piece of equipment. As previously mentioned, the more a regular bar is in front of you, the heavier it will be and the more strain it will put on your low back. This isn't always bad strain, but it can be if you overdo it or already suffer from back pain. The trap bar is a six-sided (where it gets the nickname "hex bar") piece of equipment you can step INTO and perform a deadlift. This distributes the load evenly straight down, placing a minimal amount of strain on your low back because it is much closer to your center of gravity. Most high schools will teach kids how to deadlift this way, and I have found it is much easier to teach. To top it off, most trap bar deadlifts have higher handles so you don't have to bend over as far to pick it up, making the trap bar much easier to lift than a regular deadlift.

With the trap bar, you will maintain a more upright position. The trap bar will use your quads more than a kettlebell or conventional deadlift, making it the usual preferred choice for athletes who are involved in jumping sports, such as basketball or high jump. For learning purposes, it is easier to learn and safer to get started with, which is why we recommend learning this deadlift before moving on to the conventional deadlift, the king of all hip hinges.

Chapter 5: Hip Hinge/Hip Extension (cont.)

To begin the **trap bar deadlift**, you will walk into the middle of the bar. It is important that you either use 45-pound plates OR you use bumper plates at lower weights when doing any and all deadlifts. The rubber bumper plates are all the same height as a 45-pound iron plate, which is what you want with deadlifts. That way, you are traveling the same distance each and every set.

Trap Bar Deadlift Starting Position Front View

With a trap bar deadlift, the handles are on the sides instead of straight ahead of you. You will bend over by pushing your hips back and slightly bending your knees. This is still a hip hinge. Even though your body will be more upright than it was with the kettlebell, you will still want to maintain a diagonal torso position. Following the same cues as the kettlebell deadlift, grab the floor with your feet, keep your knees out and over your ankles and feet, pull yourself to the bar, and imagine you are squeezing oranges with your armpits. This will keep full-body tension on the bar, which is very important. Keep your arms dangling like chains; do not bend your elbows to lift the weight because it will increase your risk of bicep injury.

Trap Bar Deadlift Starting Position Side View

Once in the starting position, take a big breath into your lower stomach. Brace your core around the breath. Initiate the movement by pushing the floor away from you. Once the handles have reached your knees, drive your hips forward. Squeeze your glutes together to complete the lift once you are standing straight up. To set the bar down, push your hips back until the handles reach your knees, then bend your knees/squat the rest of the way down. Once the bar has safely reached the ground, breathe out and then breathe in again to begin your next rep.

Trap Bar Deadlift Front View

Trap Bar Deadlift Side View

Chapter 5: Hip Hinge/Hip Extension (cont.)

One of the best parts about the hex bar deadlift is the versatility in its height. You can usually flip the bar over and repeat the motion from the lower, underhand position, working a greater range of motion and your hips more like a conventional deadlift.

Underhand Trap Bar Deadlift Starting Position Front View

Underhand Trap Bar Deadlift Starting Position Side View

Underhand Trap Bar Deadlift Front View

Underhand Trap Bar Deadlift Side View

Chapter 5: Hip Hinge/Hip Extension (cont.)

Deficit Hex Bar Deadlift

You can also stand on a 45-pound bumper plate to perform a **deficit hex bar deadlift**. The set up is exactly the same for these movements. The only difference being you have to bend over farther and thus work your hips through a greater range of motion, building even more hip and hamstring strength and muscle.

Deficit Hex Bar Deadlift

Barbell Hip Thrust

The **barbell hip thrust** is the king of hip extension and glute exercises. This exercise is the same as a barbell glute bridge except now your shoulders will be resting on a bench. This means your hips will bend more, which improves the stretch of your glutes. The more the stretch on a muscle, the more it will grow. This means your glutes will grow faster and stronger with the barbell hip thrust than they will the glute bridge, so it is definitely worth learning, even if it's uncomfortable at first.

You will want to find a bench that is sturdy enough not to tip over or slide. We recommend placing the bench up against a wall so it will not move. Make sure the bench has enough cushion for your upper back to rest on so that it will not cause any pain or discomfort. Load the weights onto the bar, making sure the bar is the same height using bumper plates or 45-pound plates. Once the bar is loaded, sit down next to the bench with your upper back on the side of the bench. Roll the barbell over your legs and onto your hips with the squat pad resting on your hips. Pull your feet in so your heels are about a foot away from your butt. If your legs are too close, your heels will come

Barbell Hip Thrust Starting Position

Chapter 5: Hip Hinge/Hip Extension (cont.)

off the ground during the exercise, so you'll want to correct that by moving your feet farther away. If your feet are too far away, you will feel the exercise predominantly in your hamstrings. This is mostly a glute exercise so you will need to correct this by bringing your feet in slightly. At the top of the exercise, there should be a 90-degree angle at the knee when your glutes are fully extended.

Breathe into your lower stomach and brace your core around the air. Once braced, drive your mid foot to heel into the ground with downward force. Drive your hips up toward the ceiling until you are fully extended, your shoulders to your knees being parallel with the ground. Contract your glutes for one second at the top of the exercise, squeezing them together as hard as you can. You can make this exercise harder and grow your glutes quicker by holding onto the squeeze for longer at the top. We recommend aiming for a 3-second pause at the top. Once fully extended, lower your hips back toward the ground until the weight is safely back on the ground. Be careful to control the weight on the way down going slowly. A good cadence for this exercise is 1 second up, 3-second pause, 1 second back down. Control the weight as it comes down so the weights don't slam onto the ground as loud. The stronger you get, the louder it will get to set down, but you can still control the weight to minimize the sound as best you can. Once the barbell is back on the ground, the rep is completed, and you can breathe out and breathe back in for your next rep.

Barbell Hip Thrust

Conventional Barbell Deadlift

The **conventional barbell deadlift** is the gold standard for deadlifts. It is what all serious weightlifters will talk about when talking about their max deadlift 1RM. The conventional deadlift is what you will likely use in powerlifting, CrossFit, or Olympic lifting set up competitions. The barbell deadlift will work every muscle in your posterior chain, or your whole back side, in unison and make you very good at picking up objects. This is one of the most useful skills you can have as a human being. Any manual labor job or hobby will require you to pick up heavy objects from the ground. If you are unskilled or weak in picking things up, other stronger people will have to do it for you or you will have to pay other people to do it for you. I am all about self-reliance, so it is best to learn how to pick things up on your own.

The conventional deadlift will use a bar instead of a kettlebell or hex bar. The setup is the most similar to the kettlebell deadlift that you just learned. You will walk up

Conventional Barbell Deadlift Starting Position Front View

Chapter 5: Hip Hinge/Hip Extension (cont.)

to the bar with the bar cutting an imaginary line through the midline of your feet. Your toes will be pointed either straight ahead or outward up to a 30-degree angle, exactly like the other leg exercises. You will grip the floor with your feet, keeping the weight on the mid foot in perfect unison between the three points of contact—the big toe, little toe, and heel. You will open your hips, driving your knees out so that your knees are in line with your toes, stacked perfectly on top of your ankles and feet. You will push your hips back behind you, bending over and slightly bending your knees. Once down, tuck your armpits down, imagining squeezing oranges between them. Keep your back flat and pull the slack out of your arms by keeping your chest up.

Conventional Barbell Deadlift Starting Position Side View

Once you are in the set-up position, take a deep breath into your lower stomach, bracing around the air. Initiate the movement by pushing your legs away from the ground. Once the bar has reached your knees, drive your hips forward by contracting your glutes. Keep your neck in line with the rest of your back so that when you are standing directly up, you are also looking forward. Once the rep is locked out, initiate the descent by pushing your hips back and bending over. Once the bar has reached your knees, bend your knees and squat down to finish the movement. Be very careful to imagine setting down a box of glass jars. Controlling the deadlift will unlock mounds of strength and build much more muscle mass in your glutes and hamstrings. You will see many people slam the weights down on the ground. Do not do this. You are losing progress when you do not control the weights.

Conventional Barbell Deadlift Front View

Conventional Barbell Deadlift Side View

Chapter 5: Hip Hinge/Hip Extension (cont.)

You can also stand on a 45-pound bumper plate to perform a **conventional barbell deficit deadlift**.

Conventional Barbell Deficit Deadlift

Failing a Lift

Failing a deadlift or a hip thrust is not nearly as scary as potentially failing a squat. We recommend always using clips so that the weight doesn't shift off the barbell. If you can't lift the weight, simply either set the bar back down or drop the weight if you are using bumper plates. We recommend setting it down, but if you are hurt or injured, sometimes it's best just to drop it, regardless of the noise it will make. There is no need for a spotter on either of these exercises but it can be motivating to have someone there cheering you on. Try to always use at least one pair of bumper plates on a deadlift or hip thrust. If you do have to drop the weight, this will minimize the sound and absorb the force. The iron plates will make a loud sound and you could potentially break the weights. Most gyms will have deadlift platforms where there is extra cushion so that you can set the bar down without fear of breaking any weights. If possible, set up your hip thrusts on the deadlift platform as well.

Chapter 5: Hip Hinge/Hip Extension (cont.)

Activity

Get a large notecard out and be ready to write. We're going to copy this set of deadlift cues onto the notecard so you have an easy-to-follow checklist to bring with you to the gym to make sure you're deadlifting correctly.

Deadlift Setup and Form

Stance:	Position your feet hip-width apart, with the barbell right over the middle of the feet. Your shins should be slightly touching the bar as you are bending down. Your toes should be between 0–30 degrees pointed out with your knees traveling in line, stacked on top of your ankles and feet.
Grip:	When learning to deadlift, use a double overhand grip. Once you can no longer hold on to the weight safely, purchase weightlifting chalk to add friction to help you hold on to the bar more easily. When the weight is too heavy for that grip, consider purchasing weightlifting straps or use a mixed grip as shown in the pictures.
Body Position:	Hips: Position your hips higher than a squat but lower than a stiff leg deadlift. Imagine pushing your hips back as far as you can with a slight bend in your knees.
	Spine: Keep your spine completely neutral including your neck. When you initiate the lift, you will be looking down. When you stand up with the barbell, you will be looking straight ahead. Keep your neck in line with the rest of your body.
	Shoulder Blades: Tuck your shoulder blades down and back, imagining you are squeezing an orange in between your armpits.
Breathing and Bracing:	Take a deep breath into your lower stomach and brace your core around the air. Maintain that breath and tightness throughout the lift.

Chapter 5: Hip Hinge/Hip Extension (cont.)

Key Cues for Deadlifting

Push Through the Floor:	Imagine pushing the ground away with your feet rather than pulling the bar up. This will engage your legs and hips more effectively.
Flex Your Armpits:	Imagine squeezing your armpits together as if you were squeezing an orange. This will engage your lats and keep tension on your upper body, which will improve strength and decrease injury.
Arms as Chains:	Keep your arms straight and think of them as chains holding the weight. Avoid bending your elbows while picking up the weight as this can strain your biceps.
Hip Hinge:	Focus on pushing the hips back and forth as you complete the movement. There should only be a slight bend in your knees. On the way up, push your knees straight until the bar is at the knees, and then drive your hips forward. On the way down, push your hips back until the bar reaches your knees and then bend your knees. Think to yourself "hips forward and hips back."
Shins to the Bar:	Ensure the barbell stays close to your shins and thighs as if you were dragging it across your body during the lift. This will make you stronger and decrease the likelihood of back strain.
Set the Bar Down Lightly:	Imagine you are setting down a box of glass jars. Control the weight as you go back down to set the bar down. This will work your muscles twice as hard and help you grow stronger hamstrings and hips.

Chapter 5: Hip Hinge/Hip Extension (cont.)

Get a large notecard out and be ready to write. We're going to copy this set of hip thrust cues onto the notecard so you have an easy-to-follow checklist to bring with you to the gym to make sure you're hip thrusting correctly.

Hip Thrust Setup and Form

Equipment:	Use a bench or a sturdy surface that is about knee height to support your upper back. Make sure you are either using bumper plates or 45-pound plates, as this will allow you to roll the barbell over your knees and onto your hips. If you use smaller weights, you will not be able to roll the bar over your legs. All weights must be as tall as a 45-pound weight.
Positioning:	Bench: Position the bench so it is horizontal and stable. Sit on the ground with your upper back resting against the edge of the bench.
	Barbell: Place the barbell over your hips. Use a pad or towel to cushion the bar. We highly suggest getting a squat pad and using it on the barbell to protect from bruising or hip bone pain.
Foot Placement:	Position your feet flat on the ground, hip-width apart, with your knees bent. Your feet should be close enough to your body so that your shins are vertical at the top of the movement. Your knees should make a 90-degree angle at the top.
Upper Back:	Lean back so your upper back (around the shoulder blades) is on the bench. Make sure your bench has enough cushion that it doesn't hurt your low back, but is sturdy enough to keep your upper back safely secure.

Key Cues for Hip Thrusting

Brace Your Core:	Breathe in deeply into your lower stomach and brace your core around the air to protect your spine and maintain this throughout the entire lift.
Drive Through Your Heels:	Grab the floor with your feet but primarily focus through the mid to heel portion of your feet. Drive your hips upward. This will help make sure your glutes and hamstrings are doing the work instead of your quads, protecting your low back in the process.
Squeeze Your Glutes:	At the top of the movement, fully extend your hips and squeeze your glutes hard. Your body should be a straight line from your shoulders to your knees, and you should be looking up at the ceiling.
Tuck Your Chin:	Keep your chin tucked slightly and maintain a neutral neck position. You should keep your head in line with the rest of the spine exactly like the deadlift.
Control Your Descent:	Lower your hips back to the starting position in a controlled manner. Once the bar is safely back on the ground, let your air out and rebrace for the next rep.

Chapter 6: Lunge/Step Up

Lunge/Step Up

The **lunge and step up** movement pattern is a **unilateral**, or single, leg movement involving stepping forward, backward, or to the side and either lowering your hip (lunge) or raising your hip (step up) off the ground. If you've ever bent down to tie your shoe and stood back up, then you have practiced a lunging motion. If you've ever walked up or down any steps, you have practiced a step up motion. These are movements you do 100 times a day without even thinking about them. They are incredibly important to practice and get better at because the more active you are in life, the more you will have to use this movement pattern. When you pivot to get in the way of a dribbling basketball player, you are lunging. When you move to the side to bump hard to get a spike in volleyball, you are lunging. When you are hiking, you're taking thousands of steps up. When you are taking your groceries up a flight of stairs into your apartment building, you are doing a weighted step up. These are everyday motions that will become much easier if you get stronger in these weighted lunge and step up positions.

The lunge/step up combo are incredible exercises because they load all of your weight, plus additional weight, on one leg at a time. This requires a great deal of coordination, stability, hip strength, leg strength, and balance. All of these things help your brain stay sharper, recruiting many different muscles to keep you balanced. They also work your **quadriceps** (front of the leg), **hamstrings** (back of the leg), **glutes** (butt or hips), and **core**. All of these muscles get stronger as well as the bones and other soft tissues in the low back, knee, and ankle. Your day-to-day life will get much easier as you progress in weight with these exercises. Another added benefit of these is that you do not need an entire squat rack or bench to do them. All you need is a set of dumbbells, a walking path, and some steps at home. You can get a full leg workout with very minimal equipment, making these excellent choices for home workouts as well as at the gym.

Like all of the other lower-body exercises, the same basic principles will guide you for your lunges and step ups. You will always grab the floor with your feet, practicing the short foot method to keep your foot stable; keep your knee in line with your ankle and foot, tracking with your toes; lead with the hips; and always brace before each repetition. Similar to squats and deadlifts, you will want to master the easiest exercises before progressing to the king of each variation—the walking lunge and high step up. You will learn the exercises in this sequence: split squat, reverse lunge, forward lunge, step up, and walking lunge. This will place the least amount of strain on your knees and allow you to progress appropriately to each variation of the exercise so that you become strong in various types of lunging and step up positions.

Split Squat

The **split squat** is the first and easiest to learn of the lunge variations. Your legs will stay planted once you begin your set, until completing all the reps with one leg, before moving on to the other leg to finish your set. That means if you start with your right foot forward, you will do all 10 reps of that set before bringing your right leg back and switching your left foot forward to do the next 10 reps. Because you are not stepping each and every rep like the other variations, this exercise takes the least amount of balance and coordination to learn and is a good starting point for beginners to master lunges.

Chapter 6: Lunge/Step Up (cont.)

You will begin the exercise by stepping back with one foot into a lunge position. Your feet will be hip-width apart, almost diagonal toward each other when looking down. If your right foot is forward, your left foot will be diagonal and back. You will then bend your right knee down to pick up the dumbbells off of the ground. Stand up with the weights at your side. You will inhale and take a deep breath into your lower stomach and brace your core around the breath. Keep your back straight and slightly tilted forward as you push your hips back slightly and bend your right knee down until you gently tap your left knee onto the ground. Check on your knee and make sure it is tracking with your toes, stacked on top of your ankle and foot at the bottom of the rep. Once down, you will bring your hips forward in unison as you straighten your right leg up, coming straight up to complete the lift. Once the rep is completed, take a big breath in and repeat the cycle.

Split Squat Starting Position

Split Squat

Once all of your reps are completed with your right leg, you will switch legs so that your left is forward and your right is back and diagonal and then complete the set with your left side. We recommend using knee sleeves or a pad to tap your leg onto the ground if your terrain is concrete or cement. Control the weight going up and down so that you do not slam your knee into the ground. You will want to tap your knee each time so that you know you are going low enough, getting a full range of motion each lift. If your legs are too far apart, you will over-stretch your back leg and it will not be comfortable. If your legs are too close, your heel will come up during the exercise or you will feel scrunched going back and forth. All of the weight should be on your front foot; the back foot is just there for stabilizing.

Reverse Lunge

The **reverse lunge** is the next variation of lunge that you will need to master. When you are stepping back, you place more load on your hips and hamstrings as opposed to your knee joint. This makes learning much easier and safer, as even people with some knee pain can generally do a reverse lunge. This will still strengthen the knee, but also avoid overuse or strain. The primary difference with the reverse lunge and the split squat is that after each rep, you will bring your back leg up to your neutral starting position. You will actually step back each and every lift. You can alternate legs or you can do the same leg all 10 times before switching sides to the other leg. I prefer to keep the leg the same; that way, I can get in a good rhythm and find a good position. This is what I recommend for beginners. Alternating is sometimes easier because it gives each leg a little break, but I am all about choosing the harder, more beneficial route to exercise.

Chapter 6: Lunge/Step Up (cont.)

Reverse Lunge Starting Position

Reverse Lunge

You will begin this exercise by picking up the dumbbells next to you. You will keep the dumbbells at your side during the entirety of this exercise. While standing straight up, you will take a big breath into your lower stomach and brace your core around the air. You will pick which foot you want to start with; in this case, we will stick to the right leg as your starting leg. If you are starting the work with your right leg, then your left leg will be the leg you step back with. You will pick up your left leg and step back and slightly diagonally so that your legs are still hip-width apart. As you step back, you will push your hips back in unison as you bend your right knee until your left knee gently taps the ground. Once you have tapped the ground, keeping the majority of the pressure on your right leg, step back up with your left leg and bring your left leg back to your neutral standing position. Now that you have completed one rep, you can breathe out and start the breathing sequence again to complete your set, either alternating each leg or doing all of the reps with one leg before switching over to the left leg.

Forward Lunge

Forward Lunge Starting Position Side View

Forward Lunge Starting Position Front View

The **forward lunge** is the next variation of lunge you will want to master before moving on to the step up and the walking lunge. Instead of taking a step back like with the reverse lunge, you will now take a step forward. It seems self explanatory, but the muscles it will use will be slightly different from the reverse lunge. By stepping forward, you're placing more force on the knee joint and subsequently the quad muscle. If you are prone to knee pain, this will usually hurt more. Hopefully, by

Chapter 6: Lunge/Step Up (cont.)

mastering the reverse lunge, you will be ready to take on the forward lunge without knee pain. The forward lunge is typically more athletic because usually in any sort of athletic game, you will lunge forward for the ball, not backwards. Getting to this point is important for your overall athleticism and will help make your knee joint so strong that you will not run into many issues down the road.

You will begin this exercise by picking up the dumbbells and holding them to the side of your body, standing upright and tall with your feet about hip-width apart. Prior to initiating the movement, you will take a big breath into your lower stomach and brace your core around it. Next, with your right foot (assuming you start with your right), you will step forward with a large step. You will then bend your front knee and your back knee lower into the lunge position. With your front foot, you should step and then immediately grab the floor with your feet. Your back foot will come up on its toes; do not try to keep the back foot flat-footed for ANY of the lunges. As you lunge down, stay as upright as you can with only a slight bend at the hips. This will recruit your quads much more. Make sure your knee is tracking over your toes, in alignment over your ankle and foot. As you gently tap your knee to the ground, push your front foot/right foot away from the ground, catapulting you back up to your starting position. Your left foot will only be there for added stability. Once you are standing back up into your starting position, you can release your breath and rebrace the sequence over again for your next rep. I would recommend doing all your reps on one leg before switching to the other leg to complete the set. Some weightlifting programs will have you alternate steps.

Forward Lunge Side View

Forward Lunge Front View

Step Up

Finally, after mastering the forward lunge, you will be prepared for the step up. The **step up** involves the same quad muscles as the forward lunge but is slightly less "safe" because you will be stepping onto a box. If you fail a lunge, you simply kneel down and drop the weight beside you. If you fail a step up, it's a little harder and takes a little bit more coordination to step down and put the weights down. This is why we wait to learn the step up until you've mastered the other lunges. When done correctly, the step up is an excellent functional movement that targets all the muscles in the lower body and improves balance, coordination, and cardiovascular fitness.

Picking the height of your step up is crucial. To learn the exercise, make sure the height of the box is around knee height. Make sure it is also very stable, as you will be placing your entire bodyweight and added weight onto the box. The higher the box, the more you will have to lean forward and recruit your glute muscles. The shorter the box, the more the target muscles will be your quads. To learn how to do it, start at knee height before raising the box height for high step ups.

Chapter 6: Lunge/Step Up (cont.)

Step Up Starting Position
Side View

Step Up Starting Position
Front View

Step up with your right foot firmly on the bench. Your entire foot should be on the bench, grabbing the bench as if your foot was a talon. Once securely planted, make sure your knee is in line with your toes, placed directly over the ankle and the foot. Your toes should be pointed either straight or at a slight 10- to 30-degree angle out. Next, take a deep breath into your lower stomach. Brace your core around the air. Press through the middle of your foot, focusing on foot stability until you are raised up onto the bench. Your left foot can now step up to the bench. Without breathing out, remove your left foot from the bench and slowly step down until your left leg is planted on the ground again. Breathe out and repeat with the SAME leg until the entire set is done with that leg, then switch sides to do your other leg. Too many accidents can happen when alternating feet so we recommend keeping your same foot up on the bench and stable throughout the entire set before switching to do the other side.

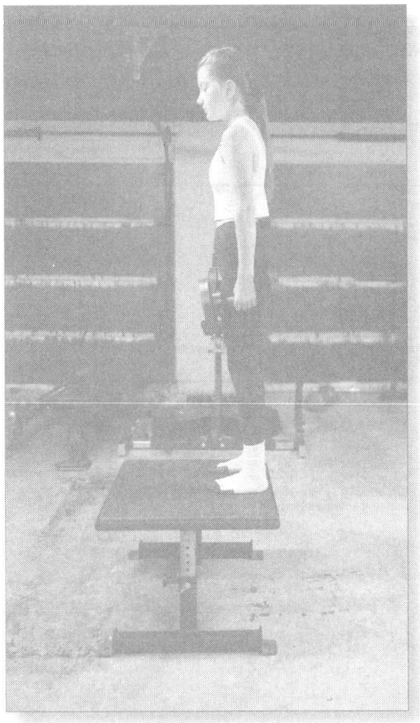

Step Up Side View

Step Up Front View

Chapter 6: Lunge/Step Up (cont.)

Walking Lunge

The **walking lunge** is the final, most athletic of the lunge variations. It is the king of lunge variations, and frankly, the most fun. If you have the space for a walking path or you are lifting on turf, this is the best overall unilateral leg exercise you can do to build total leg strength, coordination, size, balance, speed, and agility. Walking while you lunge is about as functional to real life as you can get, which is why it is our favorite athletic movement.

The walking lunge differs from the other lunges because you will alternate legs each time. You will also bring your leg back to neutral stance before alternating legs. Right foot, neutral, left foot, neutral, right foot, neutral, and repeat. Your stance will be the same as the other lunges with feet about hip-width apart. As always, breathe and brace your core around your breath to initiate the movement. You will step forward with your right foot first and immediately grip the floor with your feet like talons. As you step, you will lunge forward and down, bending both knees until your back leg touches the ground. Keeping all the weight on your front leg, push away from the ground and bring the back leg back up to your neutral starting position. Alternate legs leading with the left leg now and repeat. Make sure that your knee is traveling in line with your toes, stacked directly on top of your ankles and feet with each and every step. Keep your front toe straight or at 10 to 30 degrees, depending on individual hip anatomy. If the program calls for 10 reps, that is 10 reps on each leg. Just because you are alternating does not mean you get to do 5 reps on each leg and call it 10. You must complete 10 reps on each leg to complete the set.

Step 1 Step 2 Step 3 Step 4

Walking Lunge

Chapter 6: Lunge/Step Up (cont.)

Activity

Get a large notecard out and be ready to write. We're going to copy this set of walking lunge cues onto the notecard so you have an easy-to-follow checklist to bring with you to the gym to make sure you're lunging correctly.

Walking Lunge Setup and Form

Starting Position:	Stand tall with your feet hip-width apart. Your hands will be holding the dumbbells by your sides.
Core Engagement:	Breathe into your stomach and brace your core around the air. This will support your spine throughout the movement and prevent you from hurting your back.
Step Forward:	Take a controlled step forward with one foot. The step should be long enough so that when you lower your body, your front thigh is parallel to the ground and your back knee is just above the floor.
Knee Position:	Your knees should be traveling with the toes. You should have perfect alignment with your knee stacked directly over your ankle and foot. Grip the floor with your foot before standing back up with your other leg.
Return to Starting Position:	Bring BOTH feet back to starting position before alternating your foot and doing the other side. Do not go into another lunge without resetting the initial starting position. This will ensure that your steps are even and you do not step too close or too far away.

Key Cues for Walking Lunges

Heel-First Landing:	Step forward, landing on your heel first. This helps ensure proper knee alignment. Make sure your knee is traveling in line with your ankles and toes, either straight ahead or at a 10-degree angle out.
Lower Body:	Lower your hips until your knee gently touches the ground. Knee sleeves can be worn to minimize knee pain on any solid surfaces like concrete.
Torso Position:	Keep your back straight. If you lean forward, you will target your hips more. If you stay straight up, you will target your quads more. Either is fine as long as your back stays straight.
Drive Through Front Heel:	Push through the heel of your front foot to rise up and bring your back foot forward to the starting position. Do this at each and every rep before taking another step. That way, every rep is the same.
Forward Gaze:	Keep your gaze forward, not down, to help maintain balance and proper alignment.

Chapter 6: Lunge/Step Up (cont.)

Get a large notecard out and be ready to write. We're going to copy this set of step up cues onto the notecard so you have an easy-to-follow checklist to bring with you to the gym to make sure you're stepping up correctly.

Step Up Setup and Form

Equipment:	Use a sturdy bench, box, or step up that is knee-height or slightly higher or lower, depending on your skill. Lower will be easier and higher will require more hip flexibility. Ensure that it is stable and secure.
Starting Position:	Stand facing the bench with your feet hip-width apart. You will hold the dumbbells by your sides.
Core Engagement:	Brace your core to stabilize your torso and maintain balance throughout the lift. Do not breathe out until the lift is completed and you are back down on the ground.
Knee Alignment:	Make sure your knee on the step up is in line with your toes, stacked perfectly on top of your ankle and foot. Feet should be pointed out 0–10 degrees onto the box.
Working Foot:	Keep your front foot on the box the entire time until that set is completed before switching legs. If you are doing 10 reps, do all 10 reps with your right leg staying on the box each lift. You do not have to come back down with each rep. When you have completed all 10 reps, switch legs and do the other 10 the same way.

Key Cues for Step Ups

Foot Placement:	Place and leave your front foot doing the work firmly on the bench. Use the short foot method to keep weight evenly placed throughout the foot and keep your knee from caving in. Foot should be facing straight ahead, no more than 10 degrees out if needed.
Drive Through the Mid-Foot:	Drive through the middle of the foot, leading your body up onto the bench. That will ensure your entire leg gets worked evenly and you are balanced on the box.
Knee Alignment:	Keep your knee in line with your toes to avoid inward collapse. Your knee should be stacked on top of your ankle and foot as with all leg exercises.
Torso Position:	Either maintain an upright torso or slightly bent forward. The more bent your torso, the more of your hips you will use. The more straight, the more of your quads you will work. Either is fine, just avoid excessive lean.
Controlled Descent:	Step down slowly and under your muscular control, bring your trailing foot back to the starting position.
Leave One Foot on the Box:	Leave the foot you are doing the work with on the bench throughout the entire first half of the set. Complete all repetitions required before switching legs and doing the other side.

Chapter 7: Horizontal Push/Vertical Push

Pushing

A **pushing** exercise is an upper-body movement where the arms extend away from the body. This can be done with weights, bands, dumbbells, logs, shopping carts, doors, refrigerators, and all sorts of objects in your day-to-day life. Pushing is a real-life skill that you will need whether you're an athlete playing sports or working any sort of manual labor job. In fact, pushing objects is reported to be one of the most frequent reasons why individuals tear their rotator cuff or injure their shoulders while at work or playing sports. As previously mentioned, using weightlifting will capitalize on Wolff's Law, and Davis's Law will help strengthen your shoulder joints from the bone all the way to the tendons, ligaments, and muscles. This will allow you to live an injury-free life, improve your athleticism, and make everyday tasks that much easier.

In the first chapters on exercise, we talked about how many muscles the squat, hip hinge, hip extension, lunge, and step up used throughout your lower body. Every major muscle group in your legs can be targeted and grow in size, strength, and power just by doing one of each type of leg exercise mentioned. Pushing exercises are the same. Your upper-body muscles can be broken down into your **pectorals** (chest), **deltoids** (shoulders), **triceps** (back of your arms), the various muscles in your back (including **latissimus dorsi**, **trapezius**, **rhomboid major/minor**, and **erector spinae**), and your **biceps** (front of your arms). Pushing exercises work your chest, triceps, and the front portion of your shoulders. Pulling exercises work the various muscles of the back and your biceps. This is great because a combination of pushing and pulling exercises means every muscle in your upper body will be worked and gain strength, size, and power, and will help you remain injury-free

Pushing exercises can be further categorized into two movements: horizontal pushing and vertical pushing. **Vertical** means up and down, whereas **horizontal** means side to side. If you are standing up, you are in a vertical plane. If you are lying down, you are in a horizontal plane. If you are standing up and pushing a weight over your head, you are vertically pushing, like with an overhead press. If you are lying down on a bench and pushing the bar away from you, like a bench press, you are horizontally pressing. It is easy to imagine yourself as a compass, with your head being North, your chest being West, your legs being South, and your back being East. When you are pressing objects North, like overhead activities, you are vertically pressing (North to South directions being vertical and West to East directions being horizontal). If you are pressing an object away from you to the West, like with a dumbbell bench press or regular bench press, you are pushing in the horizontal plane. This is important because different sports require different movements, but overall, you want to make sure to work each direction of your body (North, South, East, and West). Horizontal and vertical pushing exercises are similar, but they work slightly different muscles.

Understanding the roles of different muscles during exercise helps you optimize training and prevent injuries. Movements have **prime movers** and **synergist muscles**. **Prime movers**, often called **agonist muscles**, are the primary muscles responsible for producing a specific movement. A

Chapter 7: Horizontal Push/Vertical Push (cont.)

synergist muscle is a muscle that assists the prime mover in performing the movement. It usually helps stabilize the movement and helps in keeping the muscle and joint safe during exercise. For horizontal pressing, like the **bench press**, the prime mover is the **chest (pectoralis)**. The synergist muscles would be the **back of the arms (triceps)** and **shoulders (delts)**. For vertical pressing, or pressing overhead like with an overhead press, the prime mover is the **shoulders** and the synergist muscles are the **chest** and **triceps**. Movements exercising North primarily work the shoulders with some help from the chest and triceps. Movements moving South primarily work the chest with some help from the shoulders and triceps.

This is important because the type of sport you play or muscles you want to grow with exercise will depend on the prime movers. If you are a football lineman pushing horizontally, or West, against other football players, you will most likely want to train the bench press variations. If you are a CrossFit athlete or Olympic weightlifter who presses the majority of exercises over their head, you will want to train the vertical press moving North like with an overhead press. If you throw shotput, which involves throwing at an angle, you will want to do BOTH types of pressing movements. If you want a well-rounded upper body, you will probably do two of each type of exercise within your workout.

Regardless of horizontal or vertical movement, there are some rules with all pushing exercises. With the legs, always grab the floor with your feet and make sure your knees are in line stacked evenly with your ankles and feet. With the upper-body pushing motions, you must always keep the bar in the 45-degree angle range when doing pushing or pressing movements. Whenever you grab a bar or dumbbell, you will want to imagine bending the bar down and keeping your elbows as close to your body as comfortable. By "bending the bar," you will engage your lats to help stabilize the bar or dumbbells and protect your shoulders. Oftentimes we see people doing pushups or bench pressing with their shoulders flared out. This will wear down your shoulder and lead to many shoulder injuries down the road. Grab the bar, pretend to bend the bar, and keep your elbows locked in near a 45-degree angle. If they flare out during an exercise, you are going too heavy. Following this rule will help protect your shoulders from injury.

For the purposes of learning the pushing motions, we will learn a horizontal pushing and a vertical pushing motion together before graduating to the next movements, similar to the hip hinge/hip extension combination.

Horizontal Pushing

The most common horizontal pushing motion is **pushups**. We recommend getting good at keeping your elbows locked in at 45 degrees and being able to do bodyweight pushups with ease before moving onto any weightlifting movement. If you can't perform a perfect pushup, keeping your elbows close to your body and touching your nose or chest to the ground, find a nice incline like a bench that you can work on pushups with perfect form. Do these incline pushups before moving on to a real pushup, then move on to doing weighted exercises. Master your own body before you attempt to master any weightlifting.

Horizontal pushing encompasses all bench press variations and movements. The bench press variations will all follow what is known as the **five points of contact rule**. While lying on a flat, stable bench, there will be five points of contact between the bench/ground and your body.

Chapter 7: Horizontal Push/Vertical Push (cont.)

1. Head:
   a. Keep your head FLAT on the bench. Avoid lifting your head during the lift. You will only strain your neck if your head comes off of the bench during the movement.
2. Shoulders/Upper Back
   a. Retract and squeeze your shoulder blades together. It helps to think "poke your chest out" during the bench press. You want your upper back to be on the bench but not your lower back. Your lower back should be arched, and you should be able to fit a hand in between the space in your lower back and the bench.
3. Butt/Hips
   a. Keep your hips firmly planted on the bench. DO NOT lift your hips up during the press. This can lead to lower back strain and reduced power. If your butt comes off the bench, it is too heavy of a lift for you.
4. Left Foot
   a. Plant your left foot on the floor. There are many variations of this, but we recommend learning to bench press with your feet flat on the ground.
5. Right Foot
   a. Keep your right foot firmly planted on the ground with your left. Do not let either of your legs come up off the ground during the movement.

Five points of contact is a rule for every single type of bench press, whether you're using dumbbells or at an incline or decline angle.

The next rule for horizontal pressing is to **ALWAYS lock your elbows in during the movement**. You want to grab the bar and imagine you are bending it. You will feel your lats engage, which will help stabilize the bar. When working with dumbbells, you will keep your hands at an angle, which will help keep your elbows at this 45-degree mark. If your elbows flare out, you must lower the weight. Following these rules will help you master each of the horizontal pushing exercises: the dumbbell bench press, the incline bench press, and finally, the king of horizontal pushing exercises—the barbell bench press.

Vertical Pushing

Vertical pushing involves pushing anything overhead. The shoulders are the prime mover with all vertical pushing activities, followed by the chest and triceps as synergist muscles aiding the shoulders in their work. Vertical pushing requires much more balance and stabilization of the shoulder joint, and you must be careful when pushing overhead because you don't want to drop anything onto your head. If your upper body is tight, you will definitely want to follow the upper-body mobility routine prior to any overhead movements. That means foam rolling your chest, lats, and traps, and working on your thoracic rotation and twist exercises prior to overhead pressing. Luckily, by learning the landmine and Viking press, you will be ready to master the overhead press—the king of vertical pushing exercises.

Chapter 7: Horizontal Push/Vertical Push (cont.)

Vertical pressing can be done from an upright seated position or from a standing position. Standing positions are much more athletic and applicable in real life. If you are hanging drywall overhead, chances are you will not be sitting down. For this reason, we will focus our exercises on the standing versions of vertical pushing. The seated versions can be found on the internet and are good starting points for anyone who is unable to do the standing versions or those who don't care about functional strength, specifically bodybuilders who just want bigger shoulders.

The setup for all vertical presses is the same. You will walk underneath the bar, grabbing it slightly more than shoulder-width apart. If you have poor shoulder mobility, your hands will be wider than normal. If you have normal shoulder mobility, they will be slightly more than shoulder-width apart. Your feet will always be stacked directly underneath your hips and you will always grip the floor with your feet. That will make a strong foundation for you to press from and ensure that your lower body is strong and grounded. You will unrack the bar, keeping the bar next to your collarbone. Take a couple of steps back. Once you are in a position to start, you will grab the floor with your feet and squeeze your glutes together. You will take a big breath into your lower stomach, bracing around the air as you do with all other exercises. You will then "bend the bar" in order to lock your lats into place, stabilizing your shoulders. Keeping your elbows at a 45-degree angle, you will then press the bar up, moving your head back so that the bar can pass by your chin, then moving your head forward again in a bobbing motion. You will press directly up over your head, moving the bar in a straight line. For landmine and Viking press variations, you will press through the entire movement until your shoulders and upper body are completely aligned and straight. This will make sure that your shoulder blades and upper back muscles are absorbing the force of the load, NOT your rotator cuff. This will help keep your shoulders safe and healthy for all of the pressing movements. You will descend the weight back down slowly, bobbing your chin out of the way again. Once the rep is completed and safely secure near your collarbone, you will exhale and inhale again to repeat the bracing sequence and do another rep. By following these guidelines with your vertical pressing, you will gain strength, size, power, and coordination, and improve the health and longevity of your shoulder joints.

Dumbbell Bench Press

After mastering pushups, you will likely be ready to take on the **dumbbell bench press**. Dumbbells offer greater range of motion than barbells and help even out muscle imbalances. If you are a teenager who's been playing throwing sports for years, your dominant arm is probably significantly stronger than your non-dominant arm. This muscle imbalance can cause some issues if you were to go straight into a bench press. By using dumbbells, you will have one weight in each hand. You will only be able to go as heavy as your weakest arm, which will allow that arm to catch up in strength to the other arm. If you are right-handed and you can bench a 30-pound dumbbell with your right hand but only a 20-pound dumbbell with your left, you must use 20-pound dumbbells in each hand until they can both do 30 pounds. You must always play to your weakest arm in order to avoid injury or making the muscle imbalance worse. You will not be able to go as heavy with dumbbells as it is easier to fail with them. You will simply lower the weight and push them to the side of your body onto the ground if you can no longer do a rep. This makes the dumbbell bench press perfect to learn for beginners. They also require more stabilization, balance, and coordination, helping you master these aspects of pushing before moving on to the heavier barbell exercises.

Chapter 7: Horizontal Push/Vertical Push (cont.)

To begin the dumbbell bench press, make sure you have a flat, sturdy bench to reliably lay down on. For learning purposes, you will want the bench to be flat. If it is at an incline, it will work more of your upper chest muscles. If it is at a decline, you will work more of your lower chest muscles. For learning, we recommend keeping the bench flat so you can work the middle/majority of your chest evenly. You will begin by grabbing a pair of dumbbells. You will sit down on the bench with the dumbbells resting on your knees. You will then kick up one dumbbell, using your knee to help drive the weight up to your collarbone. You will then do the same with the other dumbbell. Gently lie down with the dumbbells at your chest. Once you are safely lying down, think back to the five points of contact rule. You will stick your chest out, arching your low back. Keep your feet planted firmly on the ground. Point the dumbbells at a 45-degree angle, and make sure your elbows are at a 45-degree angle. The dumbbells should stack directly on your elbows at all times, similar to your knees stacking on top of your ankles and feet during leg exercises. This is your starting position.

Dumbbell Bench Press Starting Position

To initiate the push, you will take a deep breath into your lower stomach and brace your core around the air, exactly like you have for all of the other exercises. You will then extend your arms away from your body, pushing the dumbbells in a straight line above you and keeping in line with your nipples. You will want to think to yourself "straight up and straight back down" with all pressing movements. You will bring the dumbbells together and lightly tap each dumbbell at the top of the rep. This will completely contract your chest. Once completed, you will untap the dumbbells and bring them straight back down to your chest, making sure to actually touch the dumbbells to your chest each and every rep. Once they are down, breathe out and restart the sequence to complete another rep. When you are finished, you can either lay the dumbbells on the side of you one at a time, or you can swing your legs up and down launching your upper body up and the dumbbells back safely to your knees. This will take practice, so always start with lighter dumbbells so you can practice getting set up on and off the bench.

Dumbbell Bench Press

You should always bench press with a **spotter**, or someone to stand close by to assist you if you struggle with the lift. In this case, the spotter should keep their hands close to your wrists during the movement. If the weightlifter is struggling to get the weight up, the spotter will grab the

Chapter 7: Horizontal Push/Vertical Push (cont.)

wrists and guide them down. You must grab the wrists so that the weight doesn't accidentally fall on the weightlifter's face. If you grab the elbows, the dumbbells could crash inside toward the person's face. By grabbing the wrists, you can push the dumbbells away from the body and out of harm's way if something bad happens.

Landmine Press

The **landmine press** is a great beginner exercise focusing on the vertical pressing movement. The landmine press will involve a barbell anchored at one end (typically a **landmine attachment** in the corner of the gym). These are cheap attachments that can fit inside bumper plates, be anchored into the corner of a gym, or fit onto squat racks. Encourage your weightlifting coach or gym to get the attachment if you don't already have one. By placing the bar in the corner, you create a pivot point that allows for a variety of movements with the barbell, from rows to presses. You essentially fix the barbell to the corner, turning it into a cheap weightlifting machine rather than just an ordinary barbell. This is exactly what we want when learning to press overhead because this will add some stability to the movement while still working on your stabilizer muscles. By pressing the bar at an angle, you are also decreasing the bar weight so that most healthy people can press, whereas even overhead pressing a 45-pound bar can be hard for beginners.

Landmine Press Starting Position

The landmine press is effective for developing shoulder strength and enhancing shoulder stability. With the position and grip of the handle, it will also keep your elbow at a 45-degree angle so you won't even have to think about the elbow portion of the exercise. The landmine press is also **unilateral**, meaning it works one arm at a time. Much like the dumbbells, this gives the weightlifter an opportunity to work on muscle imbalances and fix them before moving on to the harder vertical pushing movements. This will help avoid injury down the road. Another added benefit is that this requires a great deal of core stability since the weight is only on one side of the body. This is a similar motion to javelin throwing, baseball throwing, or throwing any other object, making it the preferred pressing motion for many athletes.

Landmine Press

To perform the landmine press, set the bar up in the corner on the landmine attachment. Load the bar with whatever weight you intend on doing. If your gym has a landmine stand, you will set the bar on the stand before loading the weight. If it doesn't, you will load the weight and

Chapter 7: Horizontal Push/Vertical Push (cont.)

then have to pick up the load off the floor and into your starting position. Once in your starting position, you will stand facing the barbell corner with your feet shoulder-width apart, like all vertical pressing movements. You will hold the bar at the very end every single time. That way, the weight is distributed evenly every single rep. You will hold the barbell next to your ear off the side of your head. Grab the floor with your feet, squeeze your glutes, and take a big breath into your lower stomach and brace against the air. You will then extend your arm up over your head, slightly leaning forward at the end until your arm is straight in line with your torso, pressing the barbell directly up. Briefly pause before lowering the bar back down next to your shoulder, nearly perpendicular to your ear. Once the bar is back down, you may exhale to complete the rep and inhale/brace again before completing the next rep. Complete all reps on one arm before switching arms to complete your set.

Barbell Incline Bench Press

After mastering the dumbbells, it will be time to learn about the different angles you can incorporate to work slightly different muscle groups and introduce you to the barbell for your pressing exercises. By inclining the bench you will work the upper portion of your chest muscles, which are called the **pectoralis minor**. They are a smaller muscle group but will make your chest "pop" and become more well-rounded in muscle development. You can practice doing incline dumbbell bench presses prior to learning the barbell incline bench press if you would like.

The setup for the incline bench should only be between 30 degrees and 45 degrees on the bench. An incline any higher than a 45-degree angle will become more of a shoulder press than an incline bench press. For most benches, this will mean only moving the bench up one or two clicks. Once the height of the bench press is set, place the barbell at an appropriate height at which you will be able to comfortably rack it before and after the movement.

You will lie down on your back the same way as the flat bench, except now your upper body will be at a slight incline. You will maintain the five points of contact, keeping your head, shoulders, butt, and feet on the ground at all times. You should still have an arch at your low back, tucking your shoulder blades down and exposing as much of your chest as possible. You will grab the bar

Barbell Incline Bench Press
Starting and Ending Position

Barbell Incline Bench Press
Middle Position

Chapter 7: Horizontal Push/Vertical Push (cont.)

slightly wider than shoulder-width apart. The closer the hand positioning, the more triceps you will engage. The further the hand positioning, the more shoulders you will engage. We recommend an even approach to learn the exercises, putting the hands slightly more than shoulder-width apart. Wrap your thumbs around the bar and pretend to bend the bar, locking your elbows in place and engaging your lats to help stabilize the movement. Press up to unrack the barbell and move it directly over your chest. Once up, you will then take a deep breath into your stomach and brace around that air. Lower the barbell slowly and under control to your upper chest, right above the nipples. Keep your elbows at 45 degrees the entire time. Gently tap the bar to your chest. Extend your arms back out, pushing the weight straight above you to the starting position. Your feet should be driving into the ground while you're pressing up, which will make you a much better bench presser and allow you to incorporate your whole body into the bench press. Once the bar is back and your elbows are fully extended and locked out, exhale and reset for another rep.

A spotter for this exercise will stand behind the bar with their hands under the bar but not touching the bar. Any gentle touch can send the bar teetering in one direction or another, which makes it very unsafe for the weightlifter. Be ready to catch the bar if they need it, but try not to touch the bar unless the weightlifter asks. The weightlifter must continue pressing even after the spotter has grabbed the bar since it will likely take the combined strength of both people to lift the bar up safely if a rep is failed.

Viking Press

The **Viking press** will use the same landmine attachment as the landmine press. The Viking portion is actually a barbell attachment you will want to get. This attachment fits over the barbell so that instead of only being able to use one arm to perform a landmine press, you may now use both arms to press. The Viking attachment also allows for you to change your grip position so that your hands are now overhand while you perform the press. This is important because now you will have to keep your elbows at a 45-degree angle yourself by imagining to bend the bar as you press. The Viking press will follow the exact same cues as the landmine press, and you will push up and through the movement exactly the same as the landmine. The only difference being you now can use both arms, which will require much less core stability and coordination trying to balance your weight with one side. This means you will be able to go heavier and practice the overhand grip position, the same grip position you will need to use for the overhead press.

Viking Press Starting Position

To perform the Viking press, set the bar up in the corner on the landmine attachment. Load the bar with whatever weight you intend on doing. If your gym has a landmine stand, you will set the bar on the stand before loading the weight. If it doesn't, you will load the weight and then have to pick up the load off the floor and into your starting position. Before picking up the weight, put the **Viking attachment** on the end of the barbell, making sure it is safely secured. Most Viking press attachments

Chapter 7: Horizontal Push/Vertical Push (cont.)

will have a screw you will need to tighten into the barbell to ensure its stability. You will then lift the bar up into your starting position. This will be much easier with a stand or a box you can place the bar on for leverage. If you don't have a stand or box to lay the barbell on, recruit a gym buddy to help you get into the starting position. Once the bar is lifted up, make sure it is resting near your collarbone on your shoulders. This will be your starting position. Once in your starting position, you will stand facing the barbell corner with your feet shoulder-width apart, like all vertical pressing movements. You will be holding on to the bar in an overhand position with your elbows tucked at a 45-degree angle. Grab the floor with your feet, squeeze your glutes, and take a big breath into your lower stomach and brace against the air. You will then extend your arms up over your head, slightly leaning forward at the end until your arms are straight in line with your torso, pressing the barbell directly up. Briefly pause before lowering the bar back down to your collarbone. Once the bar is back down, you may exhale to complete the rep and inhale/brace again before completing the next rep.

Viking Press

Barbell Bench Press

Finally, after having mastered the dumbbells and incline angles of pushing movements, it is time to learn the **barbell bench press**. The barbell bench press is the king of horizontal pushing movements. It is what everyone will ask you about for your 1RM. It is also what most sports teams will heavily train and test, such as during the NFL combine. The bench press is the ultimate feat of strength for power lifters.

Luckily, the bench press is exactly like the incline bench press except at a flat bench like the dumbbell bench press. By using a barbell instead of dumbbells, you will be able to go much heavier than you ever could with dumbbells. The strength gains do come with some extra risk, however, which is why we have waited until now to learn the bench press.

Barbell Bench Press Starting and Ending Position

Set up the bench and bar height so that you can safely rack and unrack the bar. You will follow the same five points of contact for the bench press with your head, shoulders, butt, and feet all touching the bench or floor. When you get underneath the bar, make sure your eyes are level with the bar. This will help make sure you aren't too close or too far away from the bar while you're pressing. You will grab the bar slightly more than shoulder-width apart, the same as the incline bench. Grab the bar with your thumbs around the bar, "bending the bar" to engage your lats and keeping

Chapter 7: Horizontal Push/Vertical Push (cont.)

your elbows at a 45-degree angle. Unrack the bar and keep the bar in line with your middle chest/nipples. You will inhale to your lower stomach, bracing around the air. Slowly lower the bar until it is resting on your chest. Once your chest is tapped, drive your feet forward and into the ground to engage your lower body. Begin pressing the bar straight back up until your arms are fully extended and your triceps lock out the movement. Once completed, breathe out and breathe back in to complete your next rep.

Barbell Bench Press Middle Position

After the bench press is mastered, you will be able to take on any variation of bench press. Specialty bars like the kabuki bar, multi-grip bar, or other odd-shaped bars with multiple handles will be easy because the same rules apply for every bench press. By moving your hands closer for a close-grip bench press or farther away for a wide-grip bench press, you can work on different muscle parts and give yourself more variety for pressing motions. Follow the five points of contact, always lift with a spotter, and leave your ego at the door as you master the horizontal pushing movements.

Barbell Overhead Press

The **barbell overhead press** is the king of vertical pressing movements. It takes the most balance, coordination, and stabilization to press a heavy object up and over your head, which is why it is the last thing to learn of all the pushing movements. It is a fundamental exercise for building shoulder strength and stability as well as improving your upper back and core posture muscles. The barbell overhead press is an excellent exercise for any throwing athletes or anyone who works with a lot of overhead day-to-day tasks, such as painting or drywalling. The prime mover for the overhead press is your **shoulders**, aided by the synergist muscles of the **chest**, **triceps**, and **upper back**.

With the Viking press, you should have mastered the overhand position for your pressing motion. This will come in handy when completing the overhead press because your hands will also be overhand, placed slightly more than shoulder-width apart in the same position in which you learned to bench press. To set up the movement, you will set the bar on the rack at an appropriate

Front View

Side View

Barbell Overhead Press Starting Position

Chapter 7: Horizontal Push/Vertical Push (cont.)

height off which you can unrack the weight. You will set however much weight you are doing onto the bar and put clips on the bar. We recommend practicing without any weight first.

You will place your hands slightly more than shoulder-width apart and grab the bar with your thumbs wrapped around the bar. Next, you will unrack the barbell and place it next to your collarbone. "Bend the bar" and lock your lats and elbows into place, fully stabilizing your shoulders. Grip the floor with your feet and squeeze your glutes together. Next, breathe deeply into your lower stomach and brace your core around the air. You will then press overhead, bobbing your chin up and out of the way as you press directly overhead. Once your elbows are locked out and your arms are fully extended overhead in a flat line with your torso, you will begin to slowly lower the barbell back down, bobbing your head once again until the barbell is back safely resting on your shoulders near your collarbone.

Front View

Side View

Barbell Overhead Press

Chapter 7: Horizontal Push/Vertical Push (cont.)

Activity

Get a large notecard out and be ready to write. We're going to copy this set of barbell bench press cues onto the notecard so you have an easy-to-follow checklist to bring with you to the gym to make sure you're bench pressing properly.

Barbell Bench Press Setup and Form

Bench Positioning:	Ensure the bench is flat and stable. Position the bench so that the barbell is at a comfortable height to rack and unrack.
Barbell Placement:	Place the barbell on the rack at a height that allows you to easily unrack without overstretching. Load the appropriate weight plates and secure them with collars.
Body Positioning, Five Points of Contact:	Make sure your head, shoulders, butt, and feet are all safely contacting the bench or floor. You should have an arch in your lower back, large enough to fit a hand through. Think "chest high" as you retract and squeeze your shoulder blades together.
Grip:	Grasp the barbell with a grip slightly wider than shoulder-width apart. Make sure your hands are overhand and your thumbs are securely wrapped around the bar. Squeeze the bar as if you are bending it. This will place the majority of the load on the fat pads of your hands and not your wrists. Make sure your fists are straight in line with your wrists. Do not bend your wrists.

Key Cues for Barbell Bench Pressing

Unrack the Bar:	With five points of contact established, lift the bar off the rack by straightening your arms. Immediately "bend the bar" to lock your lats into place and keep your elbows at a 45-degree angle before initiating the movement. Make sure the barbell is placed over your nipple line, not your neck.
Initiate the Descent:	Breathe deeply into your stomach and brace around the air. Lower the bar in a controlled manner down to your nipple line. Make sure your elbows stay tucked near a 45-degree angle. Go down until the bar is gently touching your chest.
Initiate the Push:	Drive your feet down and forward into the ground, initiating leg drive as you push the bar straight up in as straight of a line as you can, directly above the nipple line. Lock your elbows out completely at the top of the motion to finish the rep.
Breathe Out and Reset:	Exhale once the bar has stopped moving and your elbows are locked out, securing the weight at the top of the movement. Inhale and rebrace before continuing to repeat the sequence.

Chapter 7: Horizontal Push/Vertical Push (cont.)

Activity

Get a large notecard out and be ready to write. We're going to copy this set of barbell overhead press cues onto the notecard so you have an easy-to-follow checklist to bring with you to the gym to make sure you're overhead pressing properly.

Barbell Overhead Press Setup and Form

Rack Position:	Set the barbell on a rack at about shoulder height. Ensure the rack is stable and secure. Load the appropriate weights and secure them with collars.
Body Positioning:	Stance: Stand with your feet shoulder-width apart. Your feet should be pointed straight, planted and using the short foot method, gripped to the floor.
	Grip: Grasp the barbell with a grip slightly wider than shoulder-width. Your palms should be facing forward, and your thumbs should be wrapped around the bar. "Bend the bar" with your hands so that your elbows will be locked in and your lats will stabilize the movement. Most of the pressure should be on your palm. Make sure to keep your wrists straight.
	Unrack the Bar: Lift the bar off the rack by stepping forward and positioning it at shoulder level near the collarbone. The bar should rest on your upper chest.
Initial Position:	Elbows: Keep your elbows near a 45-degree angle, locked into the movement by bending the bar. Your forearms should be vertical when viewed from the side with your elbows stacked directly beneath your wrists.
	Core: By squeezing your glutes together and bracing into your core, you will maintain core stability and prevent excess arching in your lower back. Do not arch your lower back.
	Head Position: Keep your head in a neutral position looking straight ahead.

Key Cues for Barbell Overhead Press

Pressing the Bar:	After taking your inhale and bracing your core, begin pressing the bar upward and slightly backward, bobbing your head out of the way so that the bar doesn't hit your chin. Continue pressing up until your elbows have been locked out, fully extending up over your head so that your arms are in a straight line with your torso.
Lowering the Bar:	Begin lowering the bar slowly and in a controlled manner, bobbing your head once again to avoid hitting your chin. Bring the bar back down to your upper chest, keeping your elbows near a 45-degree angle throughout the descent.
Breathe Out and Reset:	Once the bar has stopped moving, you can exhale and inhale to restart the sequence over again to perform your next rep.

Chapter 8: Horizontal Pull/Vertical Pull

Pulling

Pulling exercises involve movements where you pull a weight or resistance toward your body. Pushing exercises push away from you; pulling exercises pull toward you. As previously mentioned, pushing exercises work your chest, triceps, and shoulders. Pulling exercises work the many muscles in your back—your shoulders, biceps, and forearm muscles. If you've ever climbed a rope, pulled a heavy door, paddled in a kayak, or pulled anything toward you, you've trained the pulling movement pattern. Pulling exercises are exactly like pushing exercises in that you have two planes of movement: vertical and horizontal. With the pushing exercises, you worked your North plane by pushing things overhead like with an overhead press. You worked your Western plane by bench pressing. With pulling exercises, you will work your Southern plane doing chin-ups, pull-ups, or lat pull-downs. You will work your Eastern plane with any type of row, including chest-supported rows, dumbbell one-arm rows, and bent-over rows.

If the name of the exercise has a row in it, you can think of rowing a boat where you are seated upright and pulling toward the back of your body. A row always works the horizontal pulling plane, or your Eastern plane. Rows target the **upper back** as the prime movers, which are your **rhomboids, trapezius,** and **posterior deltoids**. Upper back just means all of the muscles right below your neck that make the shelf of your back. If the exercise has a pull-up or pull-down name in it, you are working your vertical plane, or your Southern plane. The vertical plane primarily uses your **latissimus dorsi**, or your **lat muscles**. Your lat muscles make up your V taper and are right beneath your armpit. Your **upper back** and **biceps** will be the synergist muscles in vertical plane movements.

This is important because upper back muscles are responsible for keeping your posture as you age, whereas your lats are very aesthetically pleasing and give the appearance of a larger frame. Bodybuilders traditionally spend hours working on their lats trying to get them to grow. Ignoring your rowing muscles and your upper back is a big mistake, however, because your upper back will keep your posture standing upright and tall for the rest of your life. Overall, you want an even mix between both rowing exercises and pull-down exercises to work both planes of movement evenly, which is why we will alternate exercises in order for you to master each movement, exactly how we did with pushing movements.

Horizontal Pulling

Horizontal pulling, or **rowing**, exercises will almost always focus on the upper back portion of your thoracic spine. Your **upper back** consists of your **rhomboids, trapezius,** and **posterior delts**. Your **lats (latissimus dorsi)** will also be used in rowing exercises, but they aren't the primary target for horizontal rows. Horizontal rows will help you stand more upright with better posture. Your upper back is responsible for being the base of the pyramid, or the foundation, of your neck. Keeping your upper back and posture strong will improve shoulder mobility and the stability and safety of your neck. For most daily activities, such as driving and sitting at a desk, we are hunched over a large portion of the day. This can lead to chronic back and neck pain. By strengthening your upper back, you are preventing many posture-related issues without ever having to think about your posture. Your back will just be so strong that you will always have great

Chapter 8: Horizontal Pull/Vertical Pull (cont.)

posture. This will also help your shoulders sit inside of their joint socket more evenly, preventing a lot of shoulder pain down the road.

Remember, any time you are pulling any sort of weight toward your back/behind you, or East for the visual learners, you are performing a horizontal pull. You could be seated straight up pulling against a machine and because you are pulling side to side, you are still pulling horizontally. If you are bent over completely facing the floor and pulling up, you are still performing a horizontal row because your torso is perpendicular to the floor. Inverted rows, cable rows, T-Bar rows, and bent-over rows are all examples of the horizontal pulling movements. For the purposes of this book, we will master the chest-supported row, the dumbbell one-arm row, and the king of horizontal rows: the barbell bent-over row.

Vertical Pulling

Vertical pulling or **rowing** is pulling yourself up toward a bar or pulling something down toward you. This is why we referred to vertical pulls as going in the Southern direction. You are always pulling down, whether you are moving up toward the bar like with a chin-up or you are pulling the bar down toward you like a lat pull-down. Vertical pulling works the same muscles as the horizontal pulls except there is a much greater focus on the **latissimus dorsi,** or **lats**. Remember back to your pushing exercises, your lats stabilize your shoulders as you do all pushing motions. Your lats also stabilize your deadlifts to keep your upper body flat and safe from injury when doing lower-body hip hinges.

Vertical pulls are the most practiced in bodyweight workouts. Chin-ups and pull-ups are both vertical pulls and the foundation for any back program. They can be hard to learn and may seem intimidating, so we will start with mastering the lat pull-down before moving on to chin-ups, and finally, pull-ups. With all pull-down motions, you will always lock your elbows in at a 45-degree angle prior to initiating the movement. This will stretch your lats to the greatest range of motion and improve the health and mobility of your shoulder joint. You will come to a near lockout at each and every rep so that your range of motion is the greatest. Remember, the more range of motion, the better flexibility, mobility, strength, control, and muscle you will build. When doing any sort of pulling motion, imagine you are pulling down with your elbows, not your hands. This will ensure that the majority of the work is being done by your lats and not your biceps.

Chest-Supported Dumbbell Row

The **chest-supported dumbbell row** is our favorite back exercise. This horizontal pulling variation allows for the weightlifter to lie down on their stomach on top of a slightly inclined bench. By lying down, the weightlifter does not have to worry about stabilizing their low back for the movement. Since their chest is supporting their weight, there is very little stress or risk of injury on the low back. This means you can go quite heavy in this exercise and build up a lot of upper back strength very quickly and safely. It is the most highly effective exercise for targeting the upper back muscles, the traps, rhomboids, and rear delts, while minimizing strain on the low back.

To perform this exercise, first place your dumbbells on the ground so they are easily picked up once you get into your rowing position. Set the bench at a slight incline. Many gyms will have a chest-supported row machine that you can use as well, which is the typical choice use. Most high school weight rooms will probably only have an incline bench and some dumbbells, however, so that is what we will demonstrate.

Chapter 8: Horizontal Pull/Vertical Pull (cont.)

Chest-Supported Dumbbell Row
Starting Position

Chest-Supported Dumbbell Row

After your bench is set up, lie down on the bench with your chest and abdomen supported. Your head should be at the top portion of the bench's edge. Some benches have feet support, so put your feet on the pegs if that is available. If you do not have pegs, plant your feet firmly on the floor. Grab one dumbbell at a time until you are holding both with your arms straight down, dangling like chains. You will breathe deep into your lower stomach and brace around the air. This will be harder to do while all of your body weight is lying on the bench, so this will be good practice to mastering the Valsalva maneuver technique. Retract your shoulder blades and get your chest up off the bench as much as you can. This will incorporate your **erector spinae muscles** and help prepare you for other rowing variations. Pull the weights toward your chest, focusing on squeezing your shoulder blades together. Your elbows should move up and out to the sides of your body. Pull back until your upper arm is in line with your torso. Avoid letting your chest come up off the bench. It should remain in the same position throughout the movement. After squeezing your shoulder blades together, slowly lower your arms back into the starting position. Once completed, you may exhale and inhale once again for your next rep. Keep constant chest contact, retract the shoulder blades, get your elbows to a 45-degree angle with your body, avoid momentum, and brace your core throughout the entire movement.

Lat Pull-Down

The **lat pull-down** is the first variation of the vertical pull movement pattern you will learn. It primarily focuses on the **lat muscles**, as the name gives away, which will help you with your chin-ups and pull-ups down the road. The lat pull-down is done on a cable machine, which most gyms should have access to. If your gym does not have a cable machine for lat pull-downs, skip on to band assisted chin-ups as your first vertical pull movement. The lat pull-down is one of my favorite back exercises because it can be done in a variety of ways to target the many different muscles in your back. By keeping an overhand grip, you will work your lats and upper back muscles similarly to a pull-up. If you switch your grip and do an underhand grip, you will target the lower portions of your lat muscle. By taking the bar off and using a single arm attachment, you can perform single arm lat pull-downs, which will greatly stretch your lats and improve your shoulder range of motion. For the purposes of this demonstration, we are going to focus on the overhand version of this exercise.

Chapter 8: Horizontal Pull/Vertical Pull (cont.)

First, make sure that your gym has a lat pull-down cable station with a seat and a wide-grip bar. Next, adjust the seat to the appropriate height. Do this by sitting down and making sure your knees are at a 90-degree angle with the thigh pads. Choose your starting weight. Approximately 50% of your body weight would be a good place to start. With an overhand grip, grab the handles slightly more than shoulder-width apart. Sit down while holding the bar and swing your thighs underneath the thigh pad. Let the bar stretch out your shoulders by gently leaning forward before initiating the exercise. By leaning forward and tucking your elbows forward at a 45-degree angle, you will feel a nice stretch deep into your armpits.

Back View **Side View**

Lat Pull-Down Starting Position

Next, take a deep breath into your lower stomach and brace around the air. Once braced, tilt your torso back 20 degrees as you simultaneously pull your elbows down toward the ground. By pulling your elbows down, you will effectively use your lat and other back muscles instead of overly relying on your bicep and forearm muscles. By leaning back, you will be able to pull the bar all the way down until it touches your upper chest. You must touch your upper chest for the rep to count. Once pulled down and your lats are fully squeezed, slowly let the weight go back up in a controlled manner, trying to keep your elbows at the same 45-degree angle. As you are returning to the starting position, lean forward, back to your original upright angle with your torso. It will feel like

Back View **Side View**

Lat Pull-Down

Chapter 8: Horizontal Pull/Vertical Pull (cont.)

you are rocking back and forth for this movement and that is normal. It will engage your lats and give you the best range of motion benefits as well. Once your arms are fully extended, you may exhale and inhale again to restart the next rep.

Dumbbell One-Arm Row

The **dumbbell one-arm row** is a fundamental horizontal pulling exercise for building strength in the **upper back muscles** and the **lats**. It is similar to the landmine press in the pushing motions because you will only perform one arm at a time throughout your set. This means that it will take a large degree of **core and stability muscles** to keep your torso from twisting or turning, making it a great core exercise as well. The chest-supported row had the least risk of straining your low back. The one-arm row will carry more risk because your core and low back have to hold you in the same position you were in when you were performing a chest-supported row. This means you will likely go lighter than whatever you did with the chest-supported row. To avoid groin injury, you will want to always do your one-arm rows with a tripod foot stance. The arm not doing the work will be grabbing onto an incline bench while the two legs are staggered behind, making your base for the movement. You will share equal weight distribution with your legs and the supporting arm while your other arm performs the movement.

Dumbbell One-Arm Row Starting Position

Dumbbell One-Arm Row

To set up the exercise, set your bench to an incline position. You will then place your weight next to the bench on the floor. Set your stance over shoulder-width apart with the leg opposite to the arm doing the movement slightly farther forward than your other leg. If you are doing the row with your right arm first, your right leg should be back farther than your left leg. You will bend over at the hips and place your left arm onto the top of the incline bench for support. You will brace your core and pick up the dumbbell with your right hand. Flatten your back as if thinking "perfect posture." You should be as horizontal to the ground as possible, aiming for a torso position of 45 degrees. Inhale and brace around the air in your stomach to brace your core. Begin the row by pulling your elbow back toward your body until your upper arm is in line with your torso, squeezing your lat and your upper back together. Slowly extend your arm back down to the starting position with your arm dangling like a chain. Once at the starting position, exhale and then set up for your next rep. Perform all the reps on one side before switching to the other side to finish the set.

Chapter 8: Horizontal Pull/Vertical Pull (cont.)

Chin-Up

The **chin-up** is a highly effective bodyweight exercise for building upper-body strength, particularly targeting the **lats** and the **biceps**. A chin-up is done with your palms facing you, or an **underhand position**. This underhand position allows for you to use your biceps and your back muscles. A pull-up, however, is done with an **overhand grip position**, which eliminates a lot of support from the biceps. For this reason, chin-ups are usually easier than pull-ups, and you will want to master these before progressing to pull-ups. Chin-ups can be intimidating, but they don't have to be. If you are new to them or unable to perform one, you can tie a band to the safety arms of a bench and perform the chin-ups with the assistance of a band. Most gyms will also have a weighted assistance chin-up machine so that you can get better at chin-ups by reducing your body weight using the machine. If you can do them, try to do bodyweight chin-ups. If you can do more than 10 bodyweight chin-ups with perfect form, then it's time for you to get a weight belt and add weight to your chin-ups to overload the muscle. Regardless of where you're at with the chin-ups, the body positioning and the movement is the same. The only difference would be the setup if you need a band to help, if you're doing bodyweight, or if you're adding weight. For the purposes of this book, we will demonstrate the bodyweight chin-up.

First, find a bar that allows you to perform a chin-up. Remember, your palms will be facing you with a chin-up. Jump up or grab the bar with your arms slightly more than shoulder-width apart. Allow your body to hang fully extended, dangling from your hands. Bend your knees up and cross your ankles so they don't hit the ground, which will also aid in core stability down the road. As always, take a deep breath into your stomach and brace your core around the air. To initiate the movement, pull your shoulders back and down, away from your ears. Drive your elbows toward the ground, focusing on squeezing your lats and your biceps as you move upward toward the bar. Pull yourself up until your chin is above the bar. Briefly pause before going back down, fully hanging with your arms locked back out at the bottom of the position. Let your air out and inhale again for the next rep.

Chin-Up Starting Position

Chin-Up

Barbell Bent-Over Row

The **barbell bent-over row** is the king of all rowing exercises. By using a barbell instead of dumbbells, you will be able to row much more weight, making your **upper back** and **lats** even stronger. Unfortunately, this exercise will require the most strength and stability from your core and your low back, which is why we save it until after you already have a strong low back from the one-arm row and hip hinge variations. If you are someone who skips deadlifts or legs, then

Chapter 8: Horizontal Pull/Vertical Pull (cont.)

your low back will likely be too weak to row very much. This is why you cannot take shortcuts with weightlifting. If you skip legs, your low back will suffer and then you won't be able to row as much, which means your upper back will suffer. Do not take the easy way out. Do the hard things—they're worth it.

The key to a perfect bent-over row is to be as horizontal to the ground as possible. You will do this by pushing your hips back as far as they can go, slightly bending the knees. This position is very similar to the hip hinge/deadlift position and is why having a strong deadlift will make it much easier to bend-over row heavier weight. You will set your weights up on the bar resting on the ground. You will walk over to the bar exactly the same as if you were deadlifting, walking up to the bar so the bar is drawing an imaginary line through the middle of your feet. Push your hips back and bend over, keeping a flat back, slightly bending the knees as you go down—similar to the deadlift. Grab the bar with an overhand grip and deadlift the bar to stand straight up. Once you are standing with the bar, move your hips back as if you were performing the first portion of the deadlift. Take a deep breath into the bottom of your stomach and brace your core around the air. Bend over at the hips with a slight bend in the knees for balance. Your torso should be almost parallel to the floor. Your back should remain flat. Hang your arms like chains so they are fully extended. Once you are bent over, instead of lowering the bar to the ground like a deadlift, you will pull your elbows back toward your body like the chest-supported and dumbbell one-arm rows. You will pull back to right below your sternum and right above your belly button. Once the bar touches your belly, slowly lower the weight back down as if your arms were dangling chains. Exhale and take another inhale before completing another rep.

Barbell Bent-Over Row Starting Position

Barbell Bent-Over Row

Pull-Up

The **pull-up** is the hardest vertical pulling exercise. The chin-up has the benefit of easily recruiting your biceps to help with the lift. Because of the palms forward motion, the pull-up eliminates much of the bicep help and focuses almost entirely on the back to pull you up to the bar. Rock climbing, rope climbing, or pulling yourself up safely from a cliff are all useful skills you might need someday, which is what makes pull-ups so rewarding. Most people can't do one, so working your way up to weighted pull-ups will definitely earn some respect in any gym.

Pull-Up Hand Position

Chapter 8: Horizontal Pull/Vertical Pull (cont.)

The pull-up is exactly the same as a chin-up except your hands will be in an overhand grip position. You may also use bands if you are unable to do a bodyweight pull-up on your own, or you may add weight with a belt if you can knock out 10 bodyweight pull-ups on your own. First, find a bar that allows you to perform a pull-up. Remember, your palms will be facing away from you with a pull-up. Jump up or grab the bar with your arms slightly more than shoulder width apart. Allow your body to hang fully extended, dangling from your hands. Bend your knees up and cross your ankles so they don't hit the ground, which will also aid in core stability down the road. As always, take a deep breath into your stomach and brace your core around the air. To initiate the movement, pull your shoulders back and down, away from your ears. Drive your elbows toward the ground, focusing on squeezing your lats as you move upward toward the bar. Pull yourself up until your chin is above the bar. Briefly pause before going back down, fully hanging with your arms locked back out at the bottom of the position. Let your air out and inhale again for the next rep.

Weighted Pull-Up Starting Position **Weighted Pull-Up**

Note the weight resting on the weightlifter's crossed ankles.

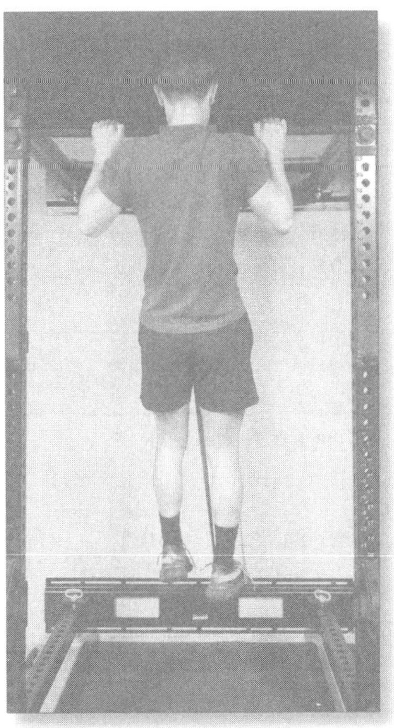

Band-Assisted Pull-Up Starting Position **Band-Assisted Pull-Up**

Note the resistance band looped around the bar and stepped into by the weightlifter.

Chapter 8: Horizontal Pull/Vertical Pull (cont.)

Activity

Get a large notecard out and be ready to write. We're going to copy this set of the barbell bent-over row cues onto the notecard so you have an easy-to-follow checklist to bring with you to the gym to make sure you're barbell rowing properly.

Barbell Bent-Over Row Setup and Form

Setup:	Choose an appropriate weight for the barbell and leave it resting on the ground, similar to a deadlift. Stand with your feet hip-width apart and toes pointed forward, gripping the ground with your feet. The bar should be cutting your feet in half with an imaginary line.
Body Positioning:	Bend at the hips and knees, keeping your back straight, similar to a deadlift. Grab the barbell with an overhand grip with your hands, slightly wider than shoulder-width apart. Deadlift the bar up to stand straight up.
Starting Position:	Bend over at the hips with a slight bend in the knees for balance. Your torso should be almost parallel to the floor. Your back should remain flat. Hang your arms like chains so they are fully extended.

Key Cues for Barbell Bent-Over Rowing

Breathe and Brace:	Take a deep breath into the bottom of your stomach and brace your core around the air.
Keep Your Back Flat:	Make sure that your hips are the only thing bending. Keep your back flat, as horizontal as you can with the ground, aiming for a 30- to 45-degree angle with your torso. Do not round your back.
Perform the Row:	Pull the barbell toward the space right below your sternum and right above your belly button. Pull your elbows back toward the ceiling and squeeze your shoulder blades together. Pull the barbell until it touches your stomach.
Lower the Row:	Slowly lower the barbell back to the starting position, dangling your arms at the bottom of the lift like chains. Maintain a flat back.
Breathe Out and Reset:	As you complete the lift, breathe out while still maintaining some tension in your core to keep you stable. Inhale and rebrace before continuing your next rep.

Chapter 9: Carry/Twist/Rotation

Carry, twist, and rotation movement patterns are fundamental patterns for functional fitness and overall body strength involving the **core** and the various layers of core muscles. Usually when people think of their core, they think of their six-pack. Well, hanging leg raises and crunches are really the two main movements you need to build up your six-pack, or your **rectus abdominis**. Unfortunately, having a six-pack won't make you more athletic and or better at moving. Very rarely in everyday life do you have to sit up, besides sitting up in bed when you wake up. That doesn't mean you shouldn't do these movements. They're great for looking good on the beach, but your primary focus for improving your athleticism and quality of life should be on exercises that focus on twisting, rotating, and your carrying capacity. They will work all the muscles within your core, your various core **fascial slings**. (These are very interesting but go beyond the scope of this book. To improve athleticism, research fascial slings and fascia-based movements.)

Carry

The **carry movement pattern** is my favorite core movement pattern to exercise. It involves holding a heavy weight, usually dumbbells, for short or long distances before setting them down. This is real-life hard training. If you've ever worked construction, worked on a farm, or even carried heavy objects like groceries down your driveway, you know how fatiguing carrying things can be. Carrying is a movement pattern that we do every day, whether it's holding a baby and walking around or lifting a wheelbarrow's handles while moving dirt for some lawn care.

Carrying targets the **abdominals**, **obliques**, **lower back**, **forearms**, **shoulders**, and **upper back**, all while dynamically moving the body. Carrying burns some serious calories while building foundational strength and making you a stronger human. It will improve your core stability, strength, balance, coordination, endurance, grip strength, posture, and mental toughness. Carrying can either be done for brief sprints with heavy weight, or for longer periods of time to focus on endurance. My favorite is to walk a set amount of distance, something like 50 yards. My favorite carrying exercises are the farmer's walk, suitcase carry, and the overhead carry.

1. **Farmer's Walk**
   a. How to perform: Hold a heavy dumbbell, kettlebell, or use a trap bar deadlift in your hands. Stand tall with your shoulders back, thinking about perfect posture. Keep your core engaged and take sips of air, trying to maintain rigidity in your core to help stabilize your spine. Walk forward for a specified distance or time.

Farmer's Walk

Chapter 9: Carry/Twist/Rotation (cont.)

   b. Benefits: Builds grip strength, core stability, and overall endurance and mental toughness.

2. **Suitcase Carry**
   a. How to perform: Hold a heavy dumbbell or kettlebell in one hand. Stand tall with your shoulders back, thinking about perfect posture. Keep your core engaged, especially your obliques, and maintain rigidity. Walk forward for a specified distance or time. Once you reach your distance or time, switch hands, turn around, and return to your starting point to complete the set.
   b. Benefits: Enhances unilateral core strength and stability. Builds grip strength, core stability, and overall endurance and mental toughness.

Suitcase Carry

3. **Overhead Carry**
   a. How to perform: Hold a weight overhead with one or both hands. If you hold with one hand, you will work the same unilateral core strength and stability that you would with the suitcase carry. If you use two, you will work the same overall core stability like with the farmer's walk. Engage your core and walk forward, maintaining an upright posture with your hands pressed straight above your head. This works best with a kettlebell flipped on the back part of your hand.
   b. Benefits: Improves shoulder stability and health, core strength, and overall balance and coordination.

Overhead Carry

Twist/Rotation

The **twisting and rotational movement pattern** involves rotating the torso around the spine. This is an essential activity for sports and for life in general. Throwing a softball, swinging a baseball bat, throwing a football, swinging a golf club, jumping and spinning in the air—almost every single sport involves twisting and rotation of the spine. When adults hurt their back, it is commonly reported that they were picking up an object and twisted the wrong way. By making your body strong in the twisting and rotational movement pattern, you can avoid many low back

Chapter 9: Carry/Twist/Rotation (cont.)

pain incidents and keep your spine and core much healthier. You will move better in life, get injured less often, and be more athletic.

The primary muscles targeted when twisting and rotating are the **obliques**, **abdominals**, **lower back**, **hip flexors**, and **hips** to stabilize your lower body. You will enhance your core strength and stability, improve rotational power and agility, and support better movement mechanics in daily activities that will help you stay healthy and make you less likely to get injured.

The exercises you pick for twisting and rotation movements depend on your goals as a weightlifter. First, you must understand the difference between power and strength. **Power** in weightlifting is how fast you can move an object, whereas **strength** is the absolute amount of resistance you can move in the movement. Jumping is an example of power because you are moving very quickly and powerfully to propel your body into the air. A leg press is an example of a strength movement where you are lifting the maximal amount of load regardless of how long it takes you to complete it. When working on power, you will do low reps and low weight but perform the movement as fast as possible. When working on strength, you do heavier loads and low reps and take longer and more controlled time with your reps. Improving power will primarily enhance your athletic abilities such as swinging a bat or throwing a javelin. Working on strength will help keep your core more stable and injury-resistant.

There are two main twisting/rotation exercises that you can perform in a variety of ways and angles: the medicine ball throw and the cable woodchopper.

1. **Medicine Ball Throw**
   a. How to perform: Stand with your feet shoulder-width apart, holding a medicine ball with both hands. Rotate your torso and throw the ball against a wall or to a partner. Use your core, leg drive, and hips to generate the power. Choose a lower weighted medicine ball that you can throw very quickly. Take a big breath before winding up to throw the ball, and breathe out only once the ball has released from your hands.
   b. Benefits: Builds power, explosive rotational strength, and athleticism.

Medicine Ball Throw

Chapter 9: Carry/Twist/Rotation (cont.)

2. **Cable Woodchopper**
   a. How to perform: Attach a handle to a high, medium, or low pulley on a cable machine. Stand with your feet shoulder-width apart. If starting from a high position, pull the handle down and across your body, holding it straight out. In a diagonal motion, engage your core and twist your torso with your core, hips, and leg drive. Move at a slow and controlled pace against the resistance of the cable machine. This can also be done with bands if your gym does not have a cable machine.
   b. Benefits: Builds rotational strength, abdominal muscle hypertrophy, and increases resiliency of the low back to help prevent injury.

Cable Woodchopper

Chapter 10: Exercise Prescription

Now that you've learned all of the major movement patterns and corresponding exercises, it's time to put it all together into your own workout regimen, or exercise prescription. The difference between a regular workout and an exercise prescription is that a regular workout is typically random and there is no method or reason to why you're doing anything. Typically, with a workout, your only goal is to work up a sweat and have fun. An **exercise prescription**, however, refers to a specific plan of fitness-related activities that are designed for a specified purpose, which is often to develop fitness, improve sports performance, rehabilitate an injury, or improve all areas of your health. An exercise prescription is essentially a plan to reach your goals, whereas an individual workout is just for fun. If you want to be successful in gaining muscle, improving your sports performance, or just staying fit and healthy, you need a good plan to follow on a month-to-month basis. All good plans come with good guiding rules to keep you on track.

Exercise Prescription Rules:

1. Work out every major movement pattern 1–2 times per week.
2. Start with the easiest-to-learn exercise in the movement pattern selection and work up every couple of months.
3. Give at least 48 hours rest in between every major movement pattern-based workout. (For example, don't work out lower body on Monday and Tuesday or on any back-to-back days. Monday and Wednesday would be acceptable, or Monday and Thursday, but give at least 48 hours of rest and recovery before working out a muscle group again.)
4. Start with low reps at the beginning of the month, and work your way up in reps each week. Keep the same weight if possible; this will ensure progressive overload is taking place.
5. Stick with the same exercises for at least two months before graduating exercises. This will ensure you maximize your potential in every exercise and become a master at all the exercises before moving on.
6. Graduate exercises every two months, or whenever you hit a plateau and are no longer able to go up in reps or weight in a specific exercise.
7. Stay well hydrated before, during, and after your workout.
8. Eat a high-protein diet on days you exercise.
9. Sleep 9–10 hours on days that you exercise.
10. Only weightlift 2–5 days per week. If you play a sport, when you're in season, lift 2 days per week to maintain muscle mass, strength, power, and coordination. When you're off season, you can resistance train up to 5 times per week.

In order to develop a plan, you must first decide how many days you can reasonably work out per week over a two-month period. Each month is called a **"mesocycle"** and collectively the two-month period is called a **"macrocycle."** If you know you can commit to working out four days, then refer back to rule number one. You want to exercise every major movement pattern 1–2 times per week. If you can work out four days, then you ideally should be able to do an upper-body

Chapter 10: Exercise Prescription (cont.)

workout, a lower-body workout, a day of rest, an upper-body workout, and a lower-body workout, followed by two more days of rest. On your upper-body days, you would horizontal push, vertical pull, vertical push, horizontal pull, and then could finish the workout with some sort of carry as your core exercise. On your lower-body days, you would squat, hip hinge or hip extension, lunge or step up, then follow with a twist and rotation exercise. By performing two upper-body and two lower-body days per week, you would be following rule number 1 and working out every major movement pattern twice each week. This would work very well if you're in the off season, don't play sports, or are just working out in the summer months.

If you are in season or busy with school and work and can only commit to two days of exercise, you would probably only have time to exercise every major muscle group one time per week. Say you can work out Monday and Thursday. You could do all of your upper-body exercises on Monday and all of your lower-body exercises on Thursday. This would still follow rule number 1 by working out every major movement pattern one time per week. If you wanted to work out three days per week, like Monday, Wednesday, and Friday, you would have the opportunity to work out most muscle groups two times per week. Monday, you would do upper body and a carry. Wednesday, you would do lower body and a twist/rotation. Friday, you would pick 4–5 of your most important exercise movement patterns and do a full-body workout. You could horizontal push, horizontal pull, squat, hip hinge, and carry. Depending on your goals, you could make this bonus day to be whatever you'd like. Football players would probably bench, squat, and deadlift, whereas perhaps baseball players would overhead press, lunge, and twist/rotate. However you'd like to set up your workouts, first just decide how many days you can commit. Then follow rules number 1 and 3 accordingly, making sure not to do workouts working the same muscle group back-to-back days.

Following rules number 2, 4, 5, and 6, start with the first exercises described in each of the chapters and stick with them for two months before graduating to the next level of exercises. This will ensure that you master the basics with every lift, and by the time you get to the most important, most beneficial exercises (barbell back squat, conventional deadlift, barbell bench press, overhead press, pull-up, and walking lunge), you will already be a master at the movement patterns and have a very easy time learning them. Your body gets used to exercises about every eight weeks, so you should make a lot of progress very fast those first eight weeks before progress slows down. This is called "the law of diminishing returns." After about eight weeks, you won't make progress as fast in a given exercise. To combat this, you will need to change exercises approximately every two months. This will ensure that you continually make progress throughout the year, never really slowing down until you've reached mastery level/advanced many years down the road.

Lastly, you will want to increase your reps each week to make sure you're doing more work than you did the previous week, following the law of progressive overload. The easiest way I have found to do this is to pick a rep scheme of 4, 6, 8, 10 or 6, 8, 10, 12, depending on your sport. If

Chapter 10: Exercise Prescription (cont.)

your sport or goals are more strength-based, you will choose 4, 6, 8, 10 reps each week. If your sport is more endurance-based, you might choose 6, 8, 10, 12 reps each week. Each week, you will do two more reps than you did the previous week. If your goal is strength and you choose the first rep scheme, week 1 you might do 3x4 at 135 pounds on squat (3 sets of 4 reps). The second week, you would want to try to do 3x6 at 135 pounds on squat. The third week, you would do 3x8 at 135 pounds on squat. Finally, in the last week of the month mesocycle, you would do, or try to do, 135 pounds for 3 sets of 10 repetitions. This last week will be your hardest week and you might need more rest in between each set of exercise. I recommend 2–4 minutes of rest in between each set of exercise. Once the first month is over, you will try to add 10–20 pounds on each lift and repeat the process. The second month you would squat 155 pounds for 4 reps week 1, then 6 reps week 2, then 8 reps week 3, then 10 reps week 4. After the second month is completed, you would change exercises.

Examples:

Ella is in gymnastics and wants to get stronger during the off season so she can jump higher and remain physically fit for when the season starts. She's never exercised on a schedule before and can dedicate two days a week to working out over the two summer months. An example of Ella's workout would be as follows:

Month 1 Day 1 Monday: Lower Body

Exercise	Week 1	Week 2	Week 3	Week 4
Goblet Box Squat	3x4 @ 20lb	3x6 @ 20lb	3x8 @ 20lb	3x10 @ 20lb
Kettlebell Deadlift	3x4 @ 30lb	3x6 @ 30lb	3x8 @ 30lb	3x10 @ 30lb
Weighted Glute Bridge	3x4 @ 45lb	3x6 @ 45lb	3x8 @ 45lb	3x10 @ 45lb
Split Squat	3x4 @ 15lb	3x6 @ 15lb	3x8 @ 15lb	3x10 @ 15lb
Medicine Ball Throw	3x4 @ 10lb	3x6 @ 10lb	3x8 @ 10lb	3x10 @ 10lb

Month 1 Day 2 Wednesday: Upper Body

Exercise	Week 1	Week 2	Week 3	Week 4
DB Bench Press	3x4 @ 20lb	3x6 @ 20lb	3x8 @ 20lb	3x10 @ 20lb
DB Chest-Supported Row	3x4 @ 20lb	3x6 @ 20lb	3x8 @ 20lb	3x10 @ 20lb
Landmine Press	3x4 @ 45lb	3x6 @ 45lb	3x8 @ 45lb	3x10 @ 45lb
Lat Pull-Down	3x4 @ 60lb	3x6 @ 60lb	3x8 @ 60lb	3x10 @ 60lb
Farmer's Walk	3x30 Yards @ 50lb	3x40 Yards @ 50lb	3x50 Yards @ 50lb	3x60 Yards @ 50lb

Chapter 10: Exercise Prescription (cont.)

Month 2 Day 1 Monday: Lower Body

Exercise	Week 1	Week 2	Week 3	Week 4
Goblet Box Squat	3x4 @ 30lb	3x6 @ 30lb	3x8 @ 30lb	3x10 @ 30lb
Kettlebell Deadlift	3x4 @ 40lb	3x6 @ 40lb	3x8 @ 40lb	3x10 @ 40lb
Weighted Glute Bridge	3x4 @ 65lb	3x6 @ 65lb	3x8 @ 65lb	3x10 @ 65b
Split Squat	3x4 @ 20lb	3x6 @ 20lb	3x8 @ 20lb	3x10 @ 20lb
Medicine Ball Throw	3x4 @ 12lb	3x6 @ 12lb	3x8 @ 12lb	3x10 @ 12lb

Month 2 Day 2 Wednesday: Upper Body

Exercise	Week 1	Week 2	Week 3	Week 4
DB Bench Press	3x4 @ 25lb	3x6 @ 25lb	3x8 @ 25lb	3x10 @ 25lb
DB Chest-Supported Row	3x4 @ 25lb	3x6 @ 25lb	3x8 @ 25lb	3x10 @ 25lb
Landmine Press	3x4 @ 50lb	3x6 @ 50lb	3x8 @ 50lb	3x10 @ 50lb
Lat Pull-Down	3x4 @ 70lb	3x6 @ 70lb	3x8 @ 70lb	3x10 @ 70lb
Farmer's Walk	3x30 Yards @ 60lb	3x40 Yards @ 60lb	3x50 Yards @ 60lb	3x60 Yards @ 60lb

As you can see, once you've decided how many days you can work out per week, you simply spread the movement patterns across those days and ensure that you are doing it 1–2 times per week. Ella picked the easiest exercises to start with and learn since she's never worked out before. Each week, she adds two more reps to her workout, keeping to the same weight each week. At the end of the first month, she goes back down to 4 reps at a heavier weight and works her way back up each week. Starting in month 3, she would keep the same plan if she continues working out twice per week, only changing the exercises. Her lower-body day would consist of the next level of difficulty exercises: the goblet squat, hex bar deadlift, weighted hip thrust, reverse lunge or step up, barbell bench press, Viking press, dumbbell one-arm row, chin-ups, suitcase carry, and cable woodchopper. It's crucial that Ella picks an appropriate weight the first week of every month. She should come close to not being able to perform another repetition, which is called **working out to failure**. You want each workout to be as hard as it can be. Assuming you are following rules 7, 8, 9, and 10, you will continue to get stronger and improve your health, allowing you to do more reps each week, almost like magic!